W9-AZP-059

Math in Focus®

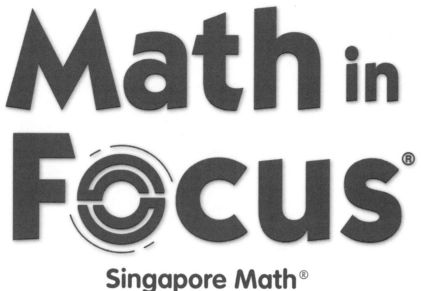

Singapore Math®
by Marshall Cavendish

Extra Practice
and Homework

Program Consultant
Dr. Fong Ho Kheong

Authors
Chelvi Ramakrishnan
Michelle Choo

Marshall Cavendish
Education

U.S. Distributor

Houghton Mifflin Harcourt.
The Learning Company™

Grade
1B

© 2020 Marshall Cavendish Education Pte Ltd

Published by Marshall Cavendish Education
Times Centre, 1 New Industrial Road, Singapore 536196
Customer Service Hotline: (65) 6213 9688
US Office Tel: (1-914) 332 8888 | Fax: (1-914) 332 8882
E-mail: cs@mceducation.com
Website: www.mceducation.com

Distributed by
Houghton Mifflin Harcourt
125 High Street
Boston, MA 02110
Tel: 617-351-5000
Website: www.hmhco.com/programs/math-in-focus

First published 2020

All rights reserved. No part of this publication may be reproduced, stored in a retrieval system or transmitted, in any form or by any means, electronic, mechanical, photocopying, recording or otherwise, without the prior written permission of Marshall Cavendish Education. If you have received these materials as examination copies free of charge, Marshall Cavendish Education retains the rights to the materials and they may not be resold. Resale of examination copies is strictly prohibited.

Marshall Cavendish® and *Math in Focus*® are registered trademarks of Times Publishing Limited.

Singapore Math® is a trademark of Singapore Math Inc.® and Marshall Cavendish Education Pte Ltd.

ISBN 978-0-358-10299-1

Printed in Singapore

4 5 6 7 8 9 10   1401   26 25 24 23 22
4500840207   B C D E F

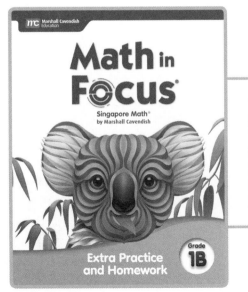

The cover image shows a koala.
Koalas have soft, grey fur and a creamy-colored chest.
They can only be found in some parts of Australia.
Koalas live on eucalyptus trees and eat the leaves.
Koalas are not bears but marsupials.
Marsupials are animals that carry their young around safely inside a pouch.

Contents

Chapter 8 **Addition and Subtraction Within 40** 1

School-to-Home Connections 1

Activity 1 Addition Without Regrouping 3

Activity 2 Addition With Regrouping 9

Activity 3 Subtraction Without Regrouping 15

Activity 4 Subtraction With Regrouping 21

Activity 5 Real-World Problems: Addition and Subtraction 27

Activity 6 Getting Ready for Multiplication 31

Math Journal 33

Put On Your Thinking Cap! 34

Chapter 9 **Length and Weight** 35

School-to-Home Connections 35

Activity 1 Comparing Lengths 37

Activity 2 Comparing More Lengths 41

Activity 3 Using a Start Line 45

Activity 4 Measuring Lengths 53

Activity 5 Measuring Length in Units 57

Activity 6 Comparing Weights 61

Activity 7 Measuring Weight 67

Activity 8 Measuring Weight in Units 71

© 2020 Marshall Cavendish Education Pte Ltd

Math Journal   **77**

Put On Your Thinking Cap!   **78**

Chapter 10 Numbers to 120   **79**

School-to-Home Connections   **79**

Activity 1 Counting to 120   **81**

Activity 2 Place Value   **87**

Activity 3 Comparing, Ordering, and
            Number Patterns   **91**

Math Journal   **97**

Put On Your Thinking Cap!   **98**

Chapter 11 Addition and Subtraction Within 100   **99**

School-to-Home Connections   **99**

Activity 1 Addition Without Regrouping   **101**

Activity 2 Addition With Regrouping   **109**

Activity 3 Subtraction Without Regrouping   **119**

Activity 4 Subtraction With Regrouping   **127**

Math Journal   **137**

Put On Your Thinking Cap!   **138**

Chapter 12 Graphs   **139**

School-to-Home Connections   **139**

Activity 1 Simple Picture Graphs   **141**

Activity 2 Tally Charts and Picture Graphs   **145**

© 2020 Marshall Cavendish Education Pte Ltd

Math Journal   **153**

Put On Your Thinking Cap!   **154**

Chapter 13 Money   **157**

School-to-Home Connections   **157**

Activity 1 Penny, Nickel, and Dime   **159**

Activity 2 Quarter   **167**

Activity 3 Counting Money   **169**

Activity 4 Adding and Subtracting Money   **175**

Math Journal   **184**

Put On Your Thinking Cap!   **185**

© 2020 Marshall Cavendish Education Pte Ltd

Preface

Welcome!

Math in Focus® : Singapore Math® *Extra Practice and Homework* is written to be used with the **Math in Focus®** : Singapore Math® *Student Edition*, to support your learning.

This book provides activities and problems that are written to closely follow what you have learned in the Student Edition.

- In **Activities**, you practice what you learned in the Student Edition, to help you master the concepts and build your confidence.

- In **MATH JOURNAL**, you share your thinking, to help you reflect on your learning.

- In **PUT ON YOUR THINKING CAP!**, you challenge yourself to apply what you have learned, as you solve the problems.

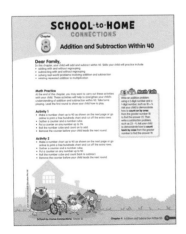

This book also includes **SCHOOL-to-HOME CONNECTIONS**. Each family letter summarizes the learning objectives and the key mathematical vocabulary you are using. The letter also includes one or more activities that your family can do with you to support your learning further.

SCHOOL-to-HOME CONNECTIONS

Chapter 8

Addition and Subtraction Within 40

Dear Family,

In this chapter, your child will add and subtract within 40. Skills your child will practice include:
- adding with and without regrouping
- subtracting with and without regrouping
- solving real-world problems involving addition and subtraction
- relating repeated addition to multiplication

Math Practice

At the end of this chapter, you may want to carry out these activities with your child. These activities will help to strengthen your child's understanding of addition and subtraction within 40. Take turns playing. Lead the first round to show your child how to play.

Activity 1
- Make a number chart up to 40 as shown on the next page or go online to print a free hundreds chart and cut off the extra rows.
- Gather a counter and a number cube.
- Put a counter on any number up to 34.
- Roll the number cube and count on to add.
- Remove the counter before your child leads the next round.

Activity 2
- Make a number chart up to 40 as shown on the next page or go online to print a free hundreds chart and cut off the extra rows.
- Gather a counter and a number cube.
- Put a counter on any number up to 40.
- Roll the number cube and count back to subtract.
- Remove the counter before your child leads the next round.

 **Math Talk**

Write an addition problem using a 2-digit number and a 1-digit number, such as 18 + 4. Ask your child to demonstrate how to **count on by ones** from the greater number 18 to find the answer 22. Then write a subtraction problem, such as 23 – 4. Ask your child to demonstrate how to **count back by ones** from the greater number to find the answer 19.

© 2020 Marshall Cavendish Education Pte Ltd

1	2	3	4	5	6	7	8	9	10
11	12	13	14	15	16	17	18	19	20
21	22	23	24	25	26	27	28	29	30
31	32	33	34	35	36	37	38	39	40

© 2020 Marshall Cavendish Education Pte Ltd

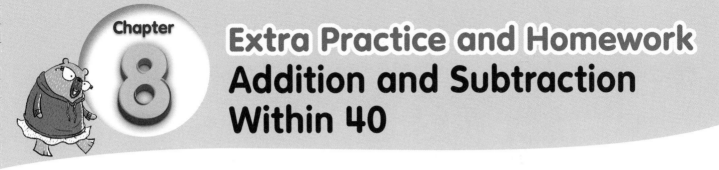

Chapter 8

Extra Practice and Homework
Addition and Subtraction Within 40

Activity 1   Addition Without Regrouping

Add.
Count on from the greater number.
Draw arrows to help you.

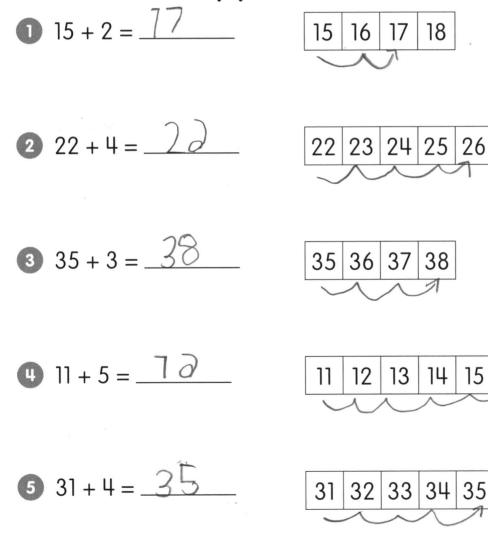

1 15 + 2 = __17__

15	16	17	18

2 22 + 4 = __22__

22	23	24	25	26

3 35 + 3 = __38__

35	36	37	38

4 11 + 5 = __72__

11	12	13	14	15	16

5 31 + 4 = __35__

31	32	33	34	35

© 2020 Marshall Cavendish Education Pte Ltd

Add.

6 $24 + 5 =$ ___29___

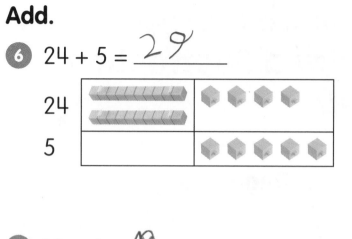

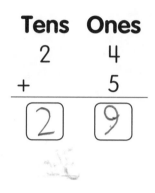

Tens	Ones
2	4
+	5
2	9

7 $12 + 6 =$ ___18___

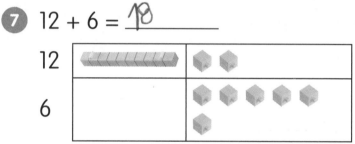

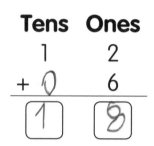

Tens	Ones
1	2
+ 0	6
1	8

Write each missing number.

8 $32 + 4 =$ ___32___

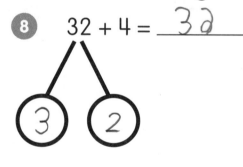

9 $11 + 8 =$ ___19___

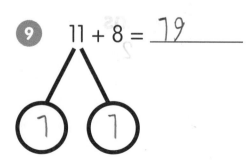

© 2020 Marshall Cavendish Education Pte Ltd

Add.
Count on from the greater number.

10 15 + 10 = _27_

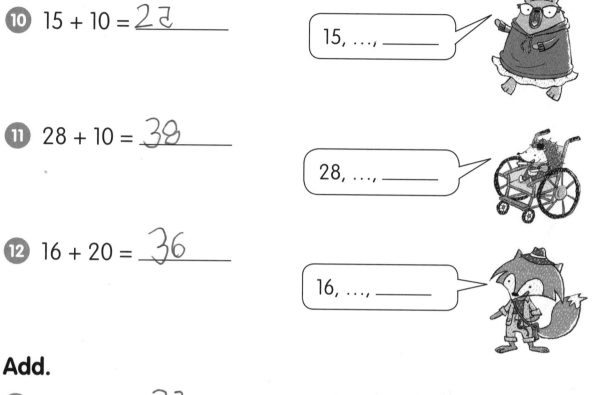

15, …, _____

11 28 + 10 = _38_

28, …, _____

12 16 + 20 = _36_

16, …, _____

Add.

13 10 + 22 = _32_

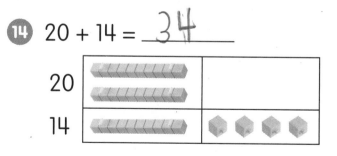

Tens	Ones
1	0
+ 2	2
3	2

14 20 + 14 = _34_

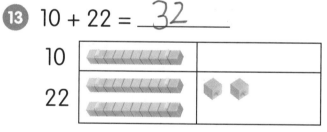

Tens	Ones
2	0
+ 1	4
3	4

© 2020 Marshall Cavendish Education Pte Ltd

Write each missing number.

15   20   +   15 = _35_

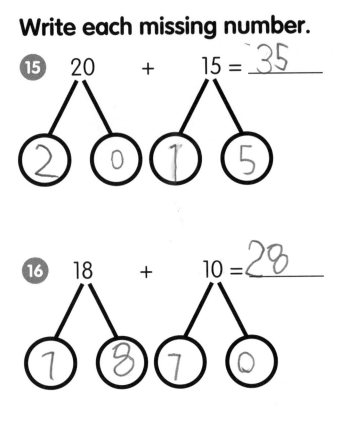

16   18   +   10 = _28_

Add.

17   13 + 23 = _32_

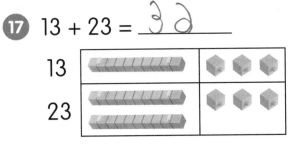

Tens	Ones
1	3
+ 2	3
3	2

18   26 + 12 = _38_

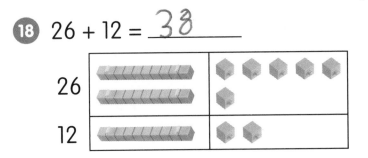

Tens	Ones
2	6
+ 1	2
3	8

© 2020 Marshall Cavendish Education Pte Ltd

Write each missing number.

19 16 + 11 = _27_

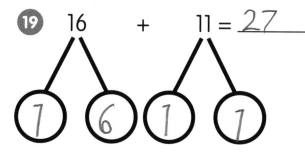

20 14 + 23 = _37_

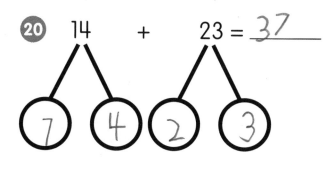

$$\begin{array}{r} 7\ 4 \\ +\ 2\ 3 \\ \hline \boxed{3}\ \boxed{7} \end{array}$$

21 24 + 14 = _38_

Tens	Ones
2	4
+ 1	4
$\boxed{3}$	$\boxed{8}$

22 21 + 17 = _38_·

Tens	Ones
2	1
+ 1	7
$\boxed{3}$	$\boxed{8}$

© 2020 Marshall Cavendish Education Pte Ltd

Add.
Then, match the answers that are the same.

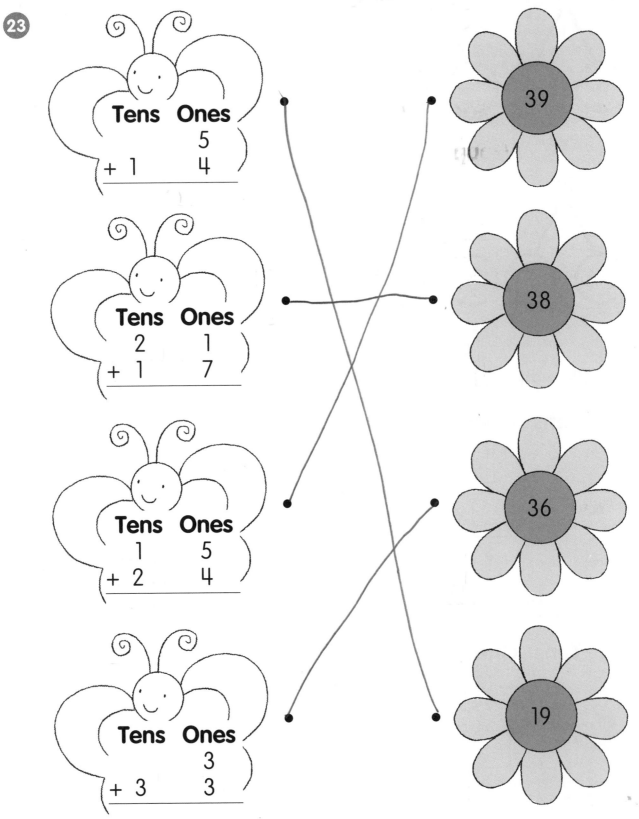

23

Tens Ones
     5
+ 1   4

Tens Ones
 2   1
+ 1   7

Tens Ones
 1   5
+ 2   4

Tens Ones
     3
+ 3   3

39

38

36

19

© 2020 Marshall Cavendish Education Pte Ltd

Extra Practice and Homework
Addition and Subtraction Within 40

Chapter 8

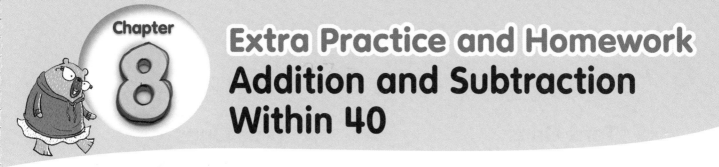

Activity 2   Addition With Regrouping

Add and regroup.

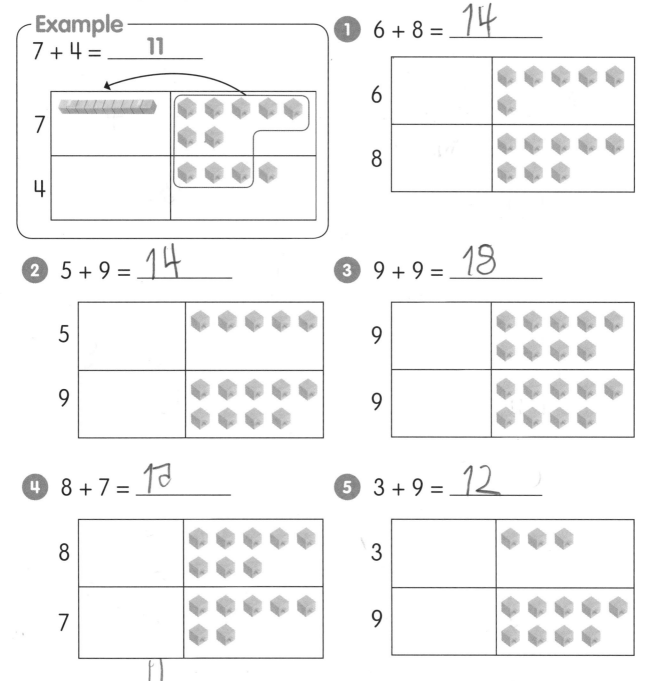

Example

7 + 4 = ____11____

1 6 + 8 = ____14____

6

8

2 5 + 9 = ____14____

5

9

3 9 + 9 = ____18____

9

9

4 8 + 7 = ____15____

8

7

5 3 + 9 = ____12____

3

9

© 2020 Marshall Cavendish Education Pte Ltd

Add.

6

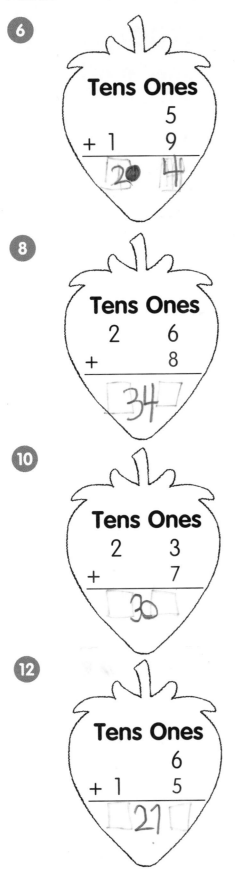

Tens Ones

```
    5
+ 1 9
-----
  2 4
```

7

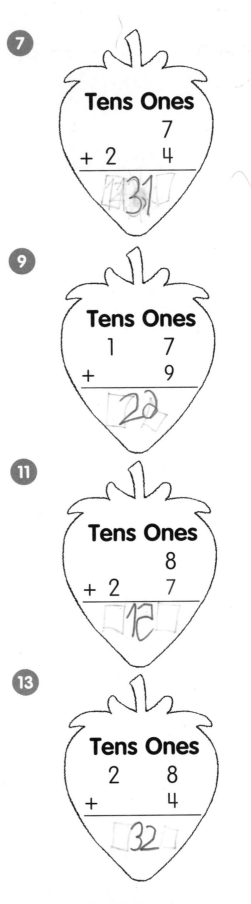

Tens Ones

```
    7
+ 2 4
-----
  31
```

8

Tens Ones

```
  2 6
+   8
-----
  34
```

9

Tens Ones

```
  1 7
+   9
-----
  2ₐ
```

10

Tens Ones

```
  2 3
+   7
-----
  3ₒ
```

11

Tens Ones

```
    8
+ 2 7
-----
  1C
```

12

Tens Ones

```
    6
+ 1 5
-----
  21
```

13

Tens Ones

```
  2 8
+   4
-----
  32
```

© 2020 Marshall Cavendish Education Pte Ltd

Add and regroup.

© 2020 Marshall Cavendish Education Pte Ltd

Example

18 + 18 = **36**

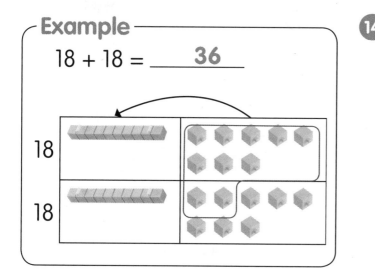

14 19 + 17 = 32

15 15 + 25 = 40

16 14 + 18 = 32

17 13 + 17 = 30

18 15 + 19 = 34

Add and regroup.

Witch ohes Defrent

19 A

Tens Ones
1   5
+ 1   8
33

20 B

Tens Ones
1   1
+ 2   9
40

21

C

Tens Ones
1   9
+ 1   9
38

22

D

Tens Ones
1   7
+ 1   6
33

youn ansar

C

Sircle the 1 Defrents.

© 2020 Marshall Cavendish Education Pte Ltd

23 Jolly Joey is finding her way back to Kelly Kangaroo.
She can only take the path that gives 30 or more.
Solve each addition sentence.
Then, trace the path that Jolly Joey can take.

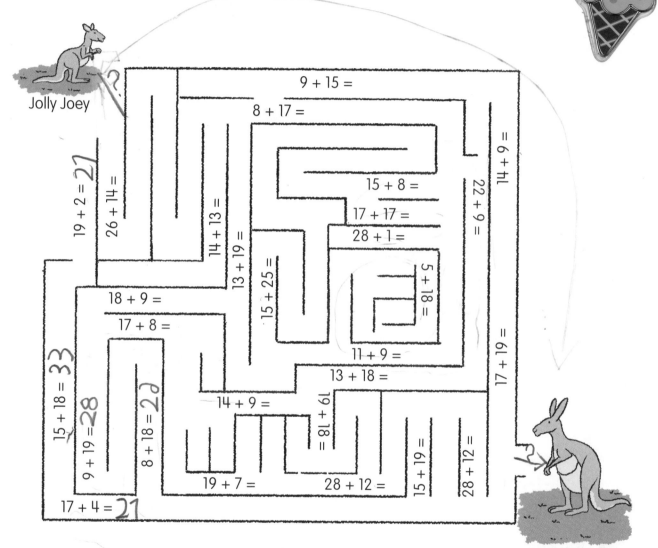

Jolly Joey

$19 + 2 = 21$

$26 + 14 =$

$9 + 15 =$

$8 + 17 =$

$14 + 9 =$

$15 + 8 =$

$17 + 17 =$

$28 + 1 =$

$14 + 13 =$

$13 + 19 =$

$15 + 25 =$

$5 + 18 =$

$18 + 9 =$

$17 + 8 =$

$11 + 9 =$

$13 + 18 =$

$15 + 18 = 33$

$9 + 19 = 28$

$8 + 18 = 2d$

$14 + 9 =$

$18 + 19 =$

$19 + 7 =$

$28 + 12 =$

$15 + 19 =$

$28 + 12 =$

$17 + 19 =$

$17 + 4 = 21$

Kelly Kangaroo

© 2020 Marshall Cavendish Education Pte Ltd

Make a 10.
Then, add.

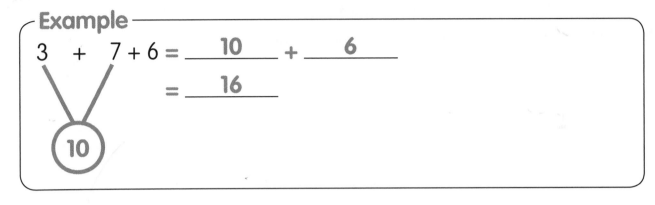

Example

$3 + 7 + 6 = \underline{\quad 10 \quad} + \underline{\quad 6 \quad}$

$= \underline{\quad 16 \quad}$

(10)

24 $3 + 7 + 9 = \underline{\qquad}$

25 $5 + 5 + 8 = \underline{\qquad}$

26 $3 + 5 + 8 = \underline{\qquad}$

27 $9 + 2 + 6 = \underline{\qquad}$

28 $9 + 9 + 5 = \underline{\qquad}$

29 $8 + 7 + 9 = \underline{\qquad}$

© 2020 Marshall Cavendish Education Pte Ltd

Name: _____ Date: _____

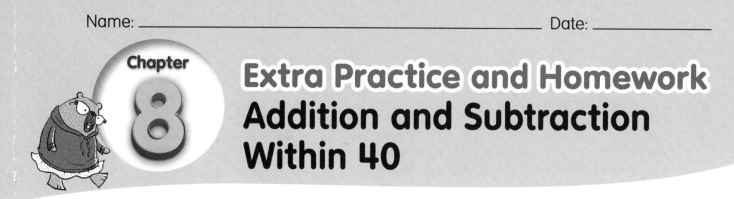

Activity 3 Subtraction Without Regrouping

Subtract.
Count back from the greater number.
Draw arrows to help you.

1. 17 − 2 = _____

| 10 | 11 | 12 | 13 | 14 | 15 | 16 | 17 |

2. 25 − 3 = _____

| 21 | 22 | 23 | 24 | 25 |

3. 39 − 3 = _____

| 31 | 32 | 33 | 34 | 35 | 36 | 37 | 38 | 39 |

4. 28 − 4 = _____

| 22 | 23 | 24 | 25 | 26 | 27 | 28 |

5. 36 − 4 = _____

| 31 | 32 | 33 | 34 | 35 | 36 |

© 2020 Marshall Cavendish Education Pte Ltd

Subtract.

6 25 – 2 = _____

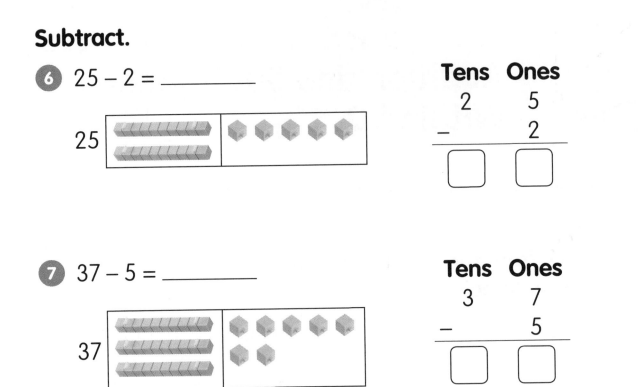

Tens	Ones
2	5
–	2
☐	☐

7 37 – 5 = _____

37

Tens	Ones
3	7
–	5
☐	☐

Write each missing number.

8   28 – 6 = _____

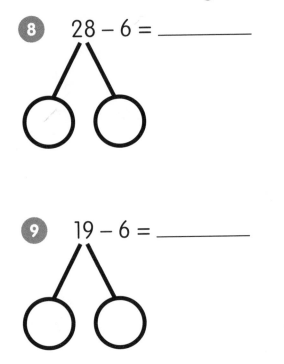

9   19 – 6 = _____

© 2020 Marshall Cavendish Education Pte Ltd

Subtract.
Count back by tens from the greater number.

10 33 – 10 = _____

33, …, _____

11 28 – 20 = _____

28 …, _____,
…, _____

12 40 – 20 = _____

40, …, _____,
…, _____

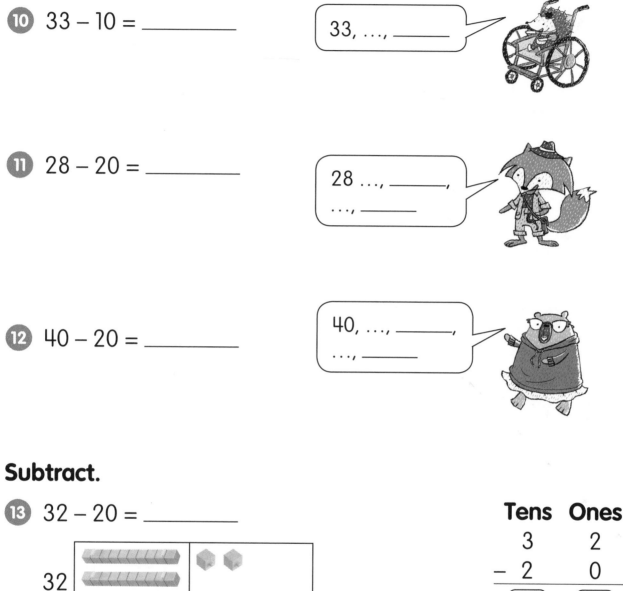

Subtract.

13 32 – 20 = _____

32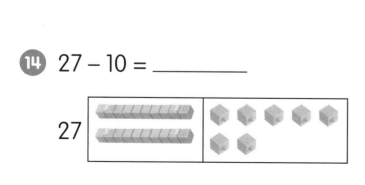

Tens	Ones
3	2
– 2	0
☐	☐

14 27 – 10 = _____

27

Tens	Ones
2	7
– 1	0
☐	☐

© 2020 Marshall Cavendish Education Pte Ltd

Write each missing number.

15 29 – 20 = _____

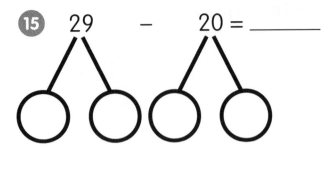

16 38 – 10 = _____

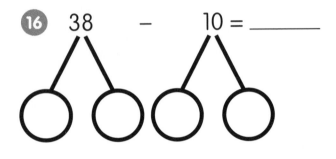

Subtract.

17 25 – 14 = _____

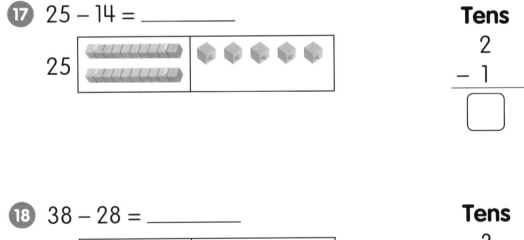

25

Tens	Ones
2	5
– 1	4
☐	☐

18 38 – 28 = _____

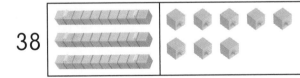

38

Tens	Ones
3	8
– 2	8
☐	☐

© 2020 Marshall Cavendish Education Pte Ltd

Write each missing number.

19 18   –   14 = _____

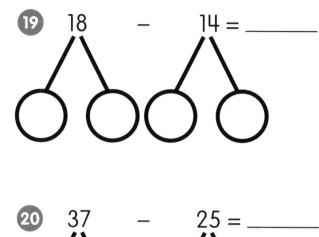

20 37   –   25 = _____

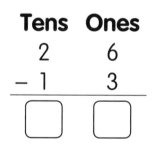

21 26 – 13 = _____

Tens	Ones
2	6
– 1	3
☐	☐

22 39 – 27 = _____

Tens	Ones
3	9
– 2	7
☐	☐

© 2020 Marshall Cavendish Education Pte Ltd

23 Sally Squirrel needs to go through the maze to get acorns.
She can only take the path that gives answers between 10 and 20.
Solve each subtraction sentence.
Then, trace the path that Sandy Squirrel can take.

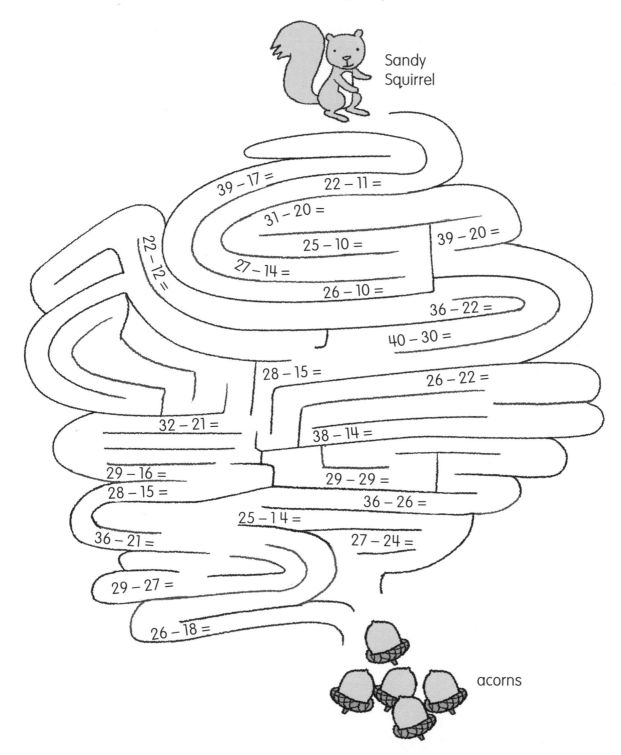

Sandy Squirrel

$39 - 17 =$

$22 - 11 =$

$31 - 20 =$

$25 - 10 =$

$39 - 20 =$

$22 - 12 =$

$27 - 14 =$

$26 - 10 =$

$36 - 22 =$

$40 - 30 =$

$28 - 15 =$

$26 - 22 =$

$32 - 21 =$

$38 - 14 =$

$29 - 16 =$

$29 - 29 =$

$28 - 15 =$

$36 - 26 =$

$25 - 14 =$

$36 - 21 =$

$27 - 24 =$

$29 - 27 =$

$26 - 18 =$

acorns

© 2020 Marshall Cavendish Education Pte Ltd

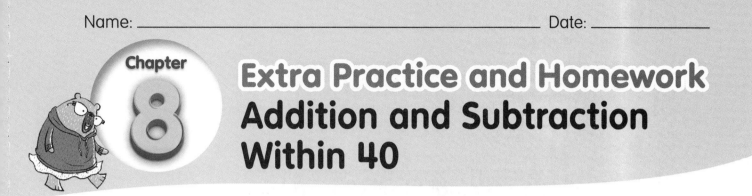

Chapter 8
Extra Practice and Homework
Addition and Subtraction Within 40

Activity 4   Subtraction With Regrouping

Regroup.
Then, complete each place-value chart.

Example

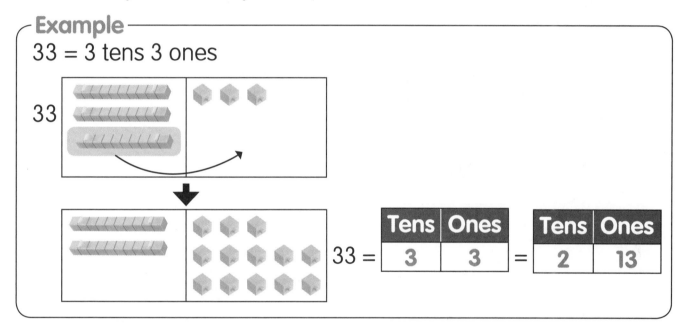

33 = 3 tens 3 ones

Tens	Ones
3	3

33 =

Tens	Ones
2	13

1 24 = _____ tens _____ ones

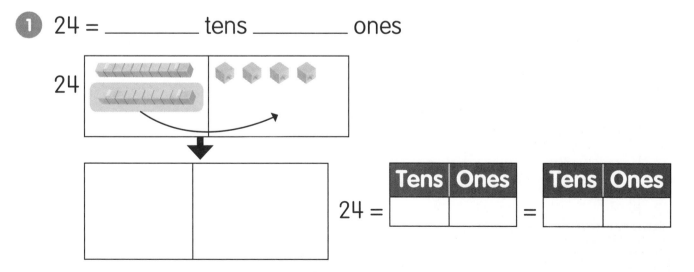

24 =

Tens	Ones

=

Tens	Ones

© 2020 Marshall Cavendish Education Pte Ltd

2

Tens	Ones

$31 =$

=

Tens	Ones

3

Tens	Ones

$27 =$

=

Tens	Ones

4

Tens	Ones

$15 =$

=

Tens	Ones

5

Tens	Ones

$30 =$

=

Tens	Ones

Regroup and subtract.

Example

$21 - 7 = ?$

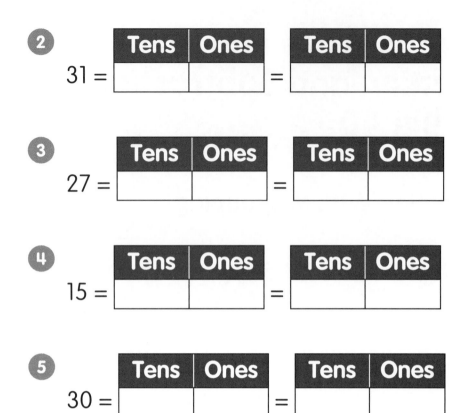

$21 = \underline{\ 1\ }$ ten $\underline{\ 11\ }$ ones

$21 - 7 = \underline{\ 14\ }$

6 $37 - 8 = ?$

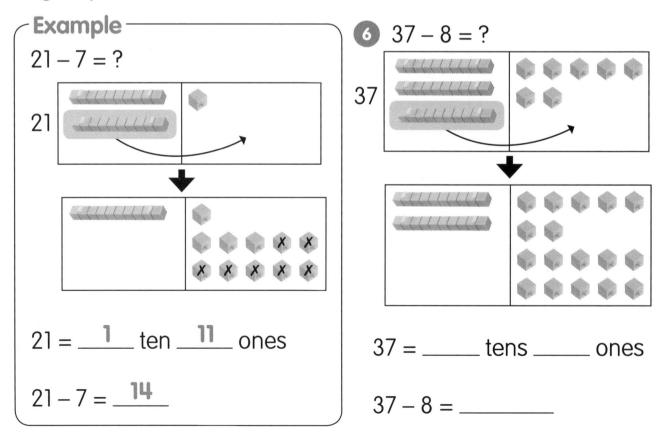

$37 = \underline{\qquad}$ tens $\underline{\qquad}$ ones

$37 - 8 = \underline{\qquad}$

© 2020 Marshall Cavendish Education Pte Ltd

7 23 − 5 = ?

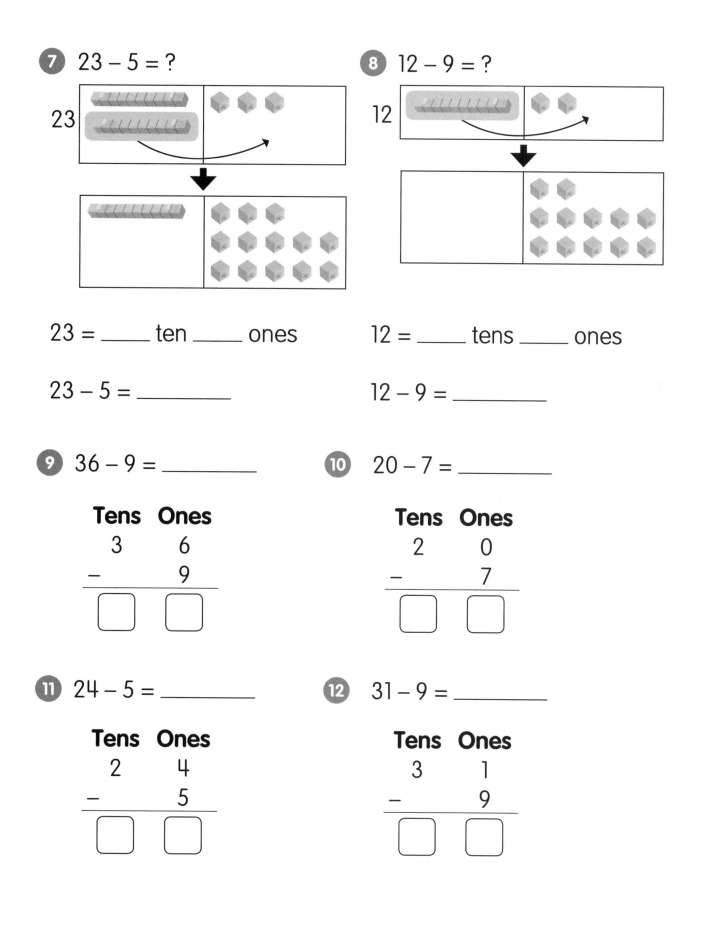

23 = _____ ten _____ ones

23 − 5 = _____

8 12 − 9 = ?

12 = _____ tens _____ ones

12 − 9 = _____

9 36 − 9 = _____

Tens	Ones
3	6
−	9
☐	☐

10 20 − 7 = _____

Tens	Ones
2	0
−	7
☐	☐

11 24 − 5 = _____

Tens	Ones
2	4
−	5
☐	☐

12 31 − 9 = _____

Tens	Ones
3	1
−	9
☐	☐

© 2020 Marshall Cavendish Education Pte Ltd

Regroup and subtract.

Example

$25 - 18 = ?$

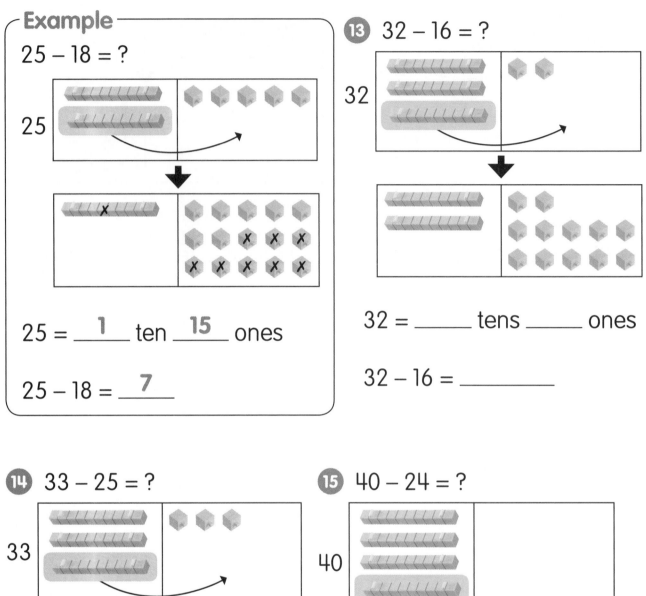

$25 = \underline{\ 1\ }$ ten $\underline{\ 15\ }$ ones

$25 - 18 = \underline{\ 7\ }$

13 $32 - 16 = ?$

$32 = \underline{\quad}$ tens $\underline{\quad}$ ones

$32 - 16 = \underline{\qquad}$

14 $33 - 25 = ?$

$33 = \underline{\quad}$ tens $\underline{\quad}$ ones

$33 - 25 = \underline{\qquad}$

15 $40 - 24 = ?$

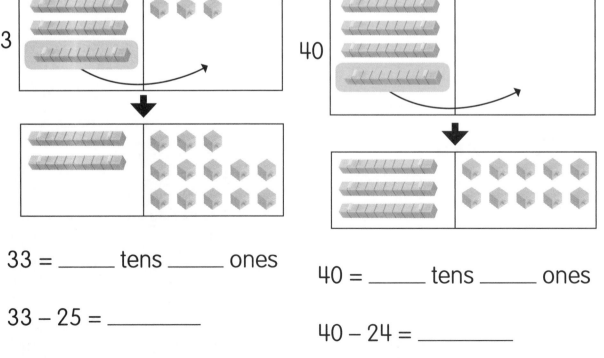

$40 = \underline{\quad}$ tens $\underline{\quad}$ ones

$40 - 24 = \underline{\qquad}$

© 2020 Marshall Cavendish Education Pte Ltd

One of these birds has green feathers.
Find out which bird it is.
Color it green.
Hint: It has an answer between 10 and 15.

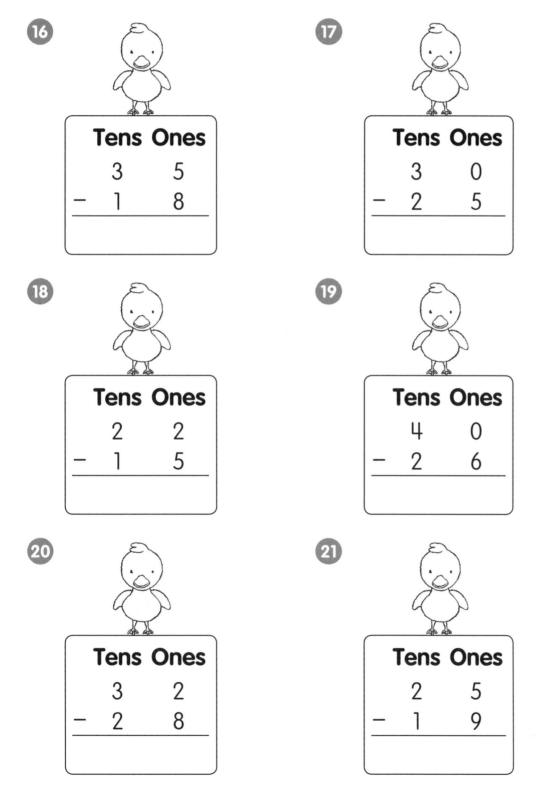

16

Tens Ones

Tens	Ones
3	5
− 1	8

17

Tens Ones

Tens	Ones
3	0
− 2	5

18

Tens Ones

Tens	Ones
2	2
− 1	5

19

Tens Ones

Tens	Ones
4	0
− 2	6

20

Tens Ones

Tens	Ones
3	2
− 2	8

21

Tens Ones

Tens	Ones
2	5
− 1	9

© 2020 Marshall Cavendish Education Pte Ltd

22 The autumn leaves below are in different colors.
If the answer is less than 5, color the leaf brown.
If the answer is 1 more than 5, color the leaf red.
If the answer is between 10 and 15, color the leaf yellow.
If the answer is greater than 20, color the leaf orange.

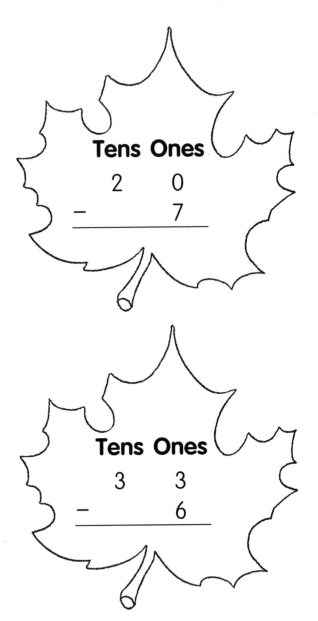

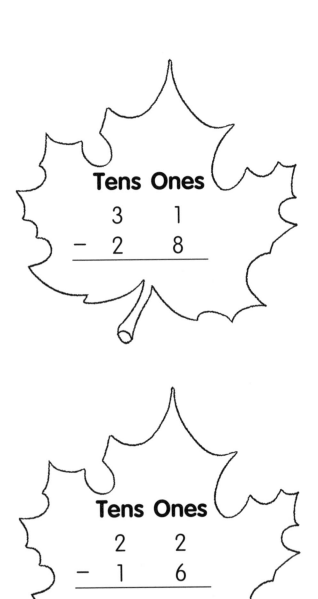

© 2020 Marshall Cavendish Education Pte Ltd

Chapter 8

Extra Practice and Homework
Addition and Subtraction Within 40

Activity 5   Real-World Problems: Addition and Subtraction

Solve.

1 Zoe has 16 postcards.
Emma has 12 postcards.
How many postcards do they have in all?

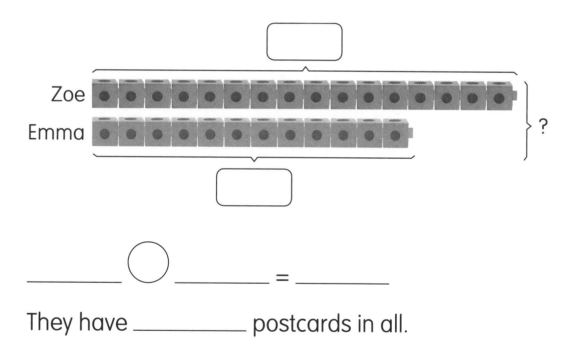

_____ ◯ _____ = _____

They have _____ postcards in all.

© 2020 Marshall Cavendish Education Pte Ltd

2 Ian had 25 glasses.
He broke 9 of them.
How many glasses had Ian left?

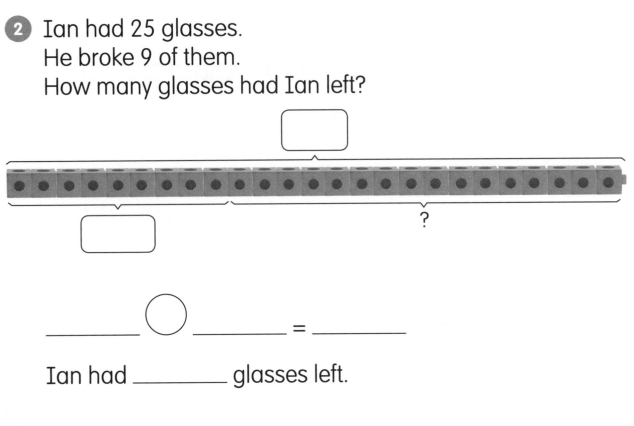

_____ ◯ _____ = _____

Ian had _____ glasses left.

3 Kate had 8 roses.
Her children gave her some roses.
She had 32 roses in all.
How many roses did her children give Kate?

Her children gave Kate _____ roses.

© 2020 Marshall Cavendish Education Pte Ltd

4 Mr Lee painted 15 chairs blue.
He painted another 16 chairs green.
How many chairs did Mr Lee paint in all?

Mr Lee painted _____ chairs in all.

5 There are 27 bullfrogs in a pond.
18 of them catch some flies for dinner.
The rest have not caught any flies.
How many bullfrogs have not caught any flies?

_____ bullfrogs have not caught any flies.

© 2020 Marshall Cavendish Education Pte Ltd

6 Lucas collected 19 leaves at a park.
John collected 21 leaves at the same park.
How many leaves did they collect in all?

They collected _____ leaves in all.

7 Angel makes 15 bracelets.
Ella makes 25 bracelets.
Who makes more bracelets?
How many more?

_____ makes _____ more bracelets than _____.

8 James has 9 toy trains.
Ali has 4 toy trains.
Isaac has 6 toy trains.
How many toy trains do the three boys have in all?

The three boys have _____ toy trains in all.

© 2020 Marshall Cavendish Education Pte Ltd

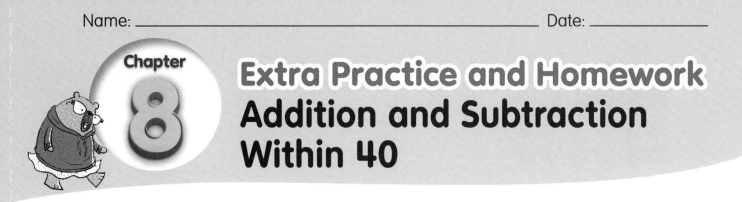

Extra Practice and Homework
Addition and Subtraction Within 40

Activity 6   Getting Ready for Multiplication

Fill in each blank.

1

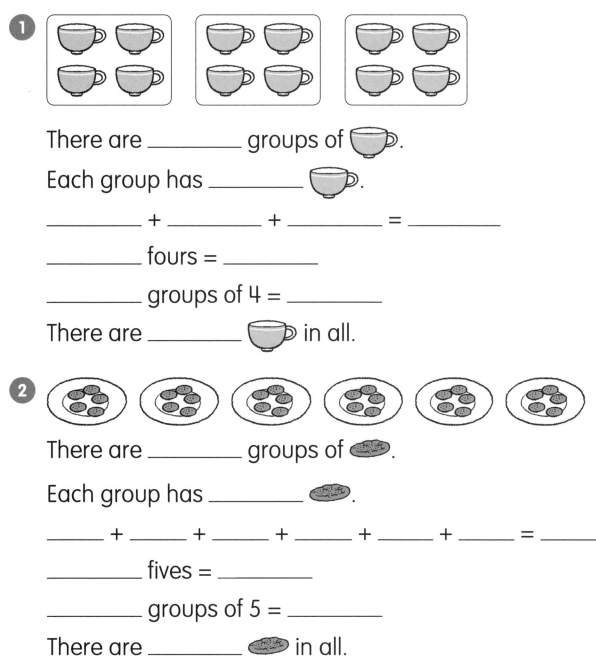

There are _____ groups of 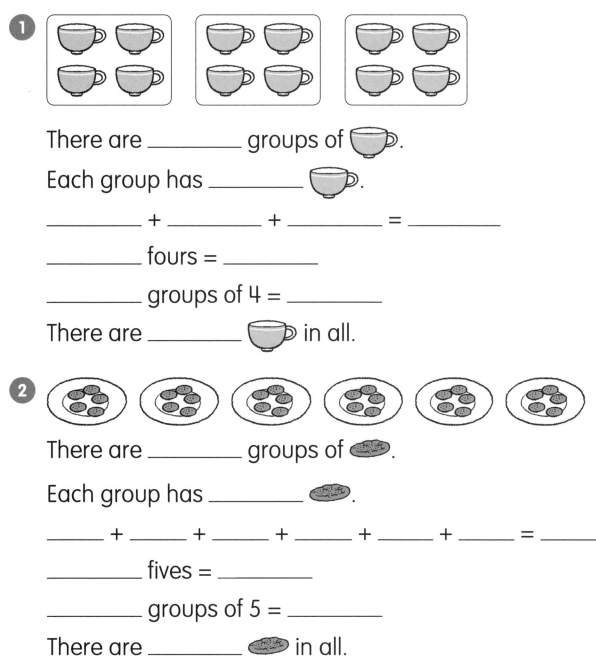.

Each group has _____ 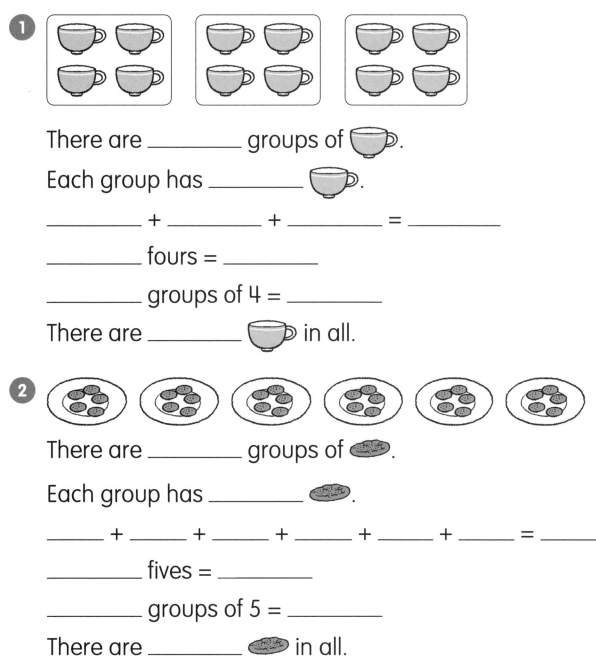.

_____ + _____ + _____ = _____

_____ fours = _____

_____ groups of 4 = _____

There are _____ in all.

2

There are _____ groups of .

Each group has _____ .

____ + ____ + ____ + ____ + ____ + ____ = ____

_____ fives = _____

_____ groups of 5 = _____

There are _____ in all.

© 2020 Marshall Cavendish Education Pte Ltd

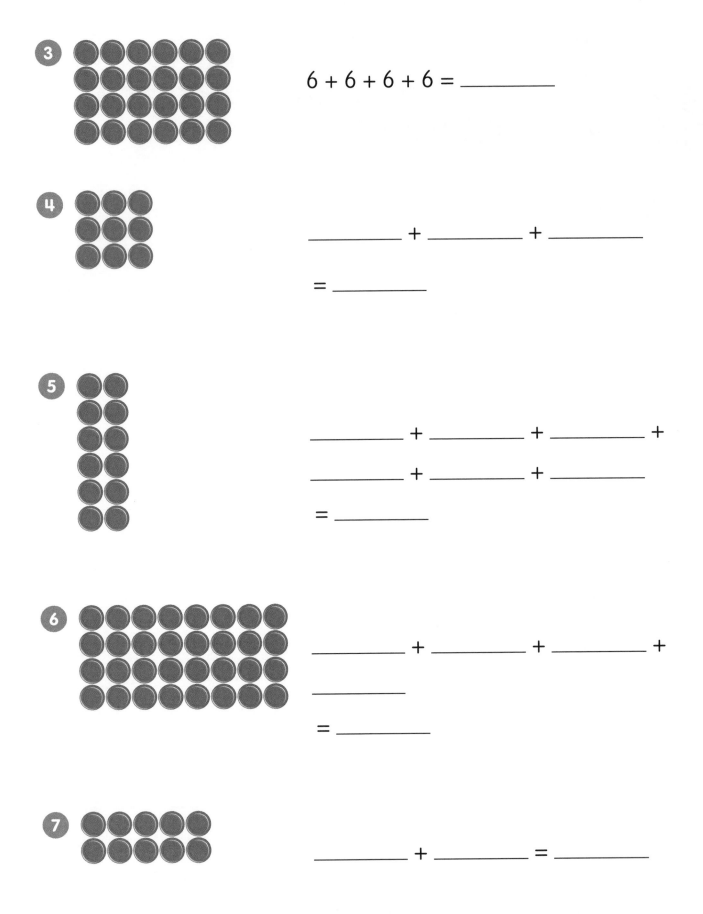

3

$6 + 6 + 6 + 6 = $ _____

4

_____ + _____ + _____

= _____

5

_____ + _____ + _____ +

_____ + _____ + _____

= _____

6

_____ + _____ + _____ +

_____

= _____

7

_____ + _____ = _____

© 2020 Marshall Cavendish Education Pte Ltd

Mathematical Habit 2 Use mathematical reasoning

Look at the problem and the table.
Some sentences in the table are correct.
Tick (✓) the correct sentences.

Alex has 21 storybooks.
He read 16 storybooks.
How many storybooks has he not read?

☐	Alex has 16 storybooks.
☐	Alex read 16 storybooks.
☐	Alex has 21 storybooks.
☐	Alex read 21 storybooks.
☐	I subtract 16 from 21 to find the answer.
☐	I add 16 and 21 to find the answer.
☐	16 + 21 = 37
☐	21 − 16 = 6
☐	Alex has not read 5 storybooks.
☐	Alex has not read 36 storybooks.

© 2020 Marshall Cavendish Education Pte Ltd

Mathematical Habit 1 Persevere in solving problems

1 Think of two pairs of 2-digit numbers that add up to 30.
Write two addition sentences.

_____ + _____ = 30

_____ + _____ = 30

Mathematical Habit 1 Persevere in solving problems

2 Think of two pairs of 2-digit numbers.
When I subtract each pair of numbers, I get 30.
Write two subtraction sentences.

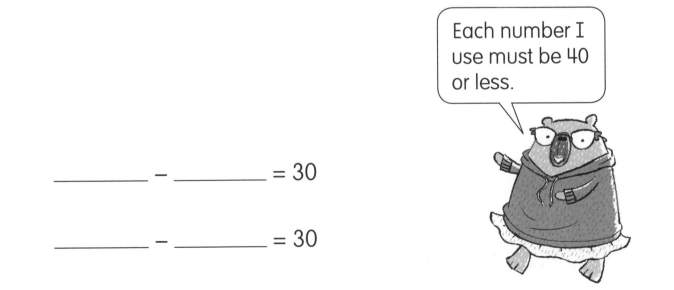

Each number I use must be 40 or less.

_____ – _____ = 30

_____ – _____ = 30

© 2020 Marshall Cavendish Education Pte Ltd

SCHOOL-to-HOME
CONNECTIONS

Length and Weight

Dear Family,

In this chapter, your child will measure lengths and weights. Skills your child will practice include:

- comparing lengths
- measuring lengths using non-standard and standard units
- comparing weights
- measuring weights using non-standard and standard units

Math Practice

At the end of this chapter, you may want to carry out these activities with your child. These activities will help to strengthen your child's understanding of length and weight. You will use **non-standard units** of measurement, such as everyday objects.

Activity 1

- Gather paper clips or straws to help your child practice measuring and comparing lengths using non-standard units.
- Gather 3 similar objects to measure, such as cereal boxes of different sizes.
- Have your child use the units you choose to measure the length and height of the boxes and order them first by length, and then by height.

Math Talk

Look for objects in your home that you can use to engage your child in a discussion of **length**, or the distance from one end of an object to the other end, and **weight**, or how heavy or light an object is. Use the words **tall, taller, tallest, short, shorter, shortest, long, longer,** and **longest** in your discussion, as well as **light, lighter, lightest, heavy, heavier,** and **heaviest**.

© 2020 Marshall Cavendish Education Pte Ltd

Activity 2

- Gather a coat hanger, 2 identical plastic cups, 2 equal lengths of string, tape, a pencil, and a heavy book to make a balance.
- Punch holes on opposite sides of each cup and use string to make a handle. Loop the cup handles over opposite ends of the coat hanger and secure them tightly.
- Hang the coat hanger over a doorknob.
- Choose some objects to weigh.
- Have your child predict and then test which objects are lighter or heavier.

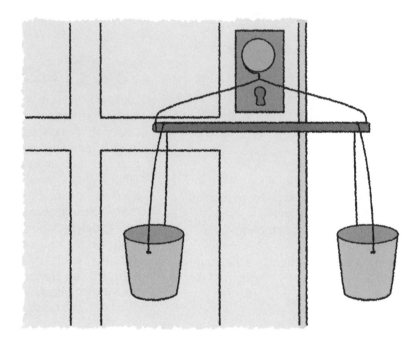

© 2020 Marshall Cavendish Education Pte Ltd

Chapter 9
Extra Practice and Homework
Length and Weight

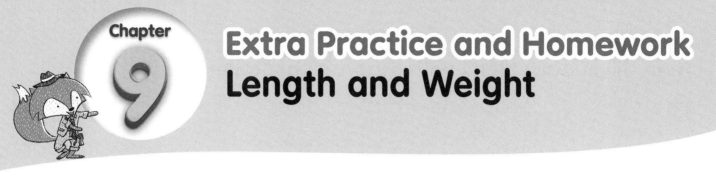

Activity 1 Comparing Lengths

Look at each picture.
Then, circle the correct answer.

1 Which is longer?

2 Who is taller?

3 Which is shorter?

© 2020 Marshall Cavendish Education Pte Ltd

Look at each picture.
Then, fill in each blank with "shorter" or "taller."

4

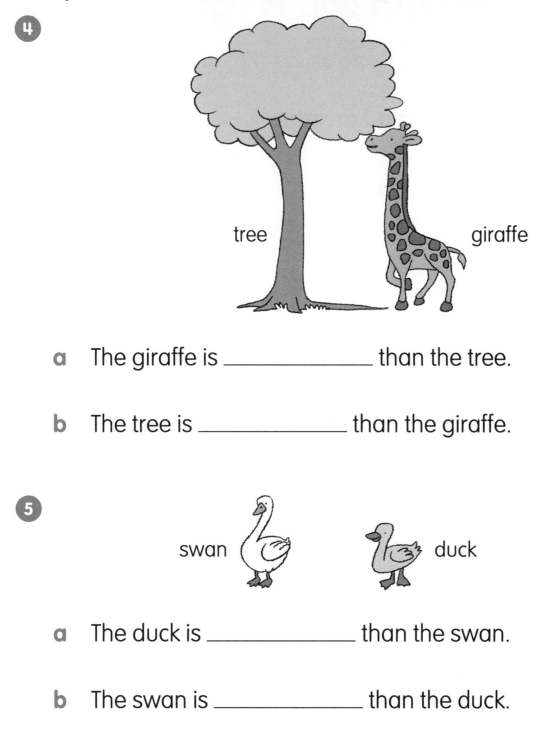

tree   giraffe

a   The giraffe is _____ than the tree.

b   The tree is _____ than the giraffe.

5

swan   duck

a   The duck is _____ than the swan.

b   The swan is _____ than the duck.

© 2020 Marshall Cavendish Education Pte Ltd

Look at each picture.
Then, fill in each blank with "longer" or "shorter."

6

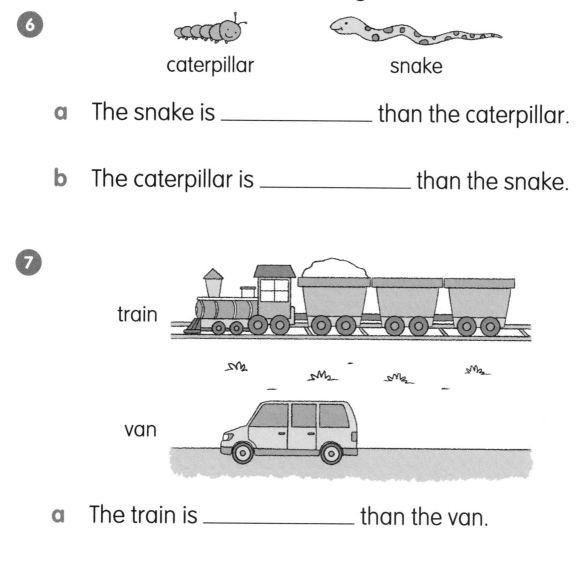

caterpillar   snake

a   The snake is _____ than the caterpillar.

b   The caterpillar is _____ than the snake.

7

train

van

a   The train is _____ than the van.

b   The van is _____ than the train.

© 2020 Marshall Cavendish Education Pte Ltd

Draw.

Example

A longer arrow

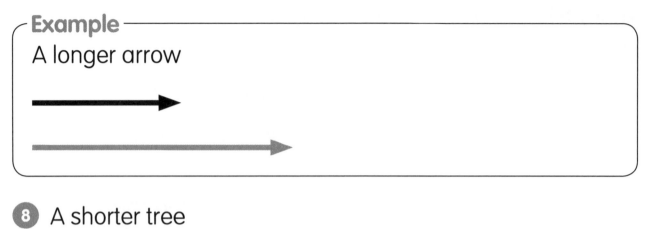

---

8 A shorter tree

9 A taller ship

© 2020 Marshall Cavendish Education Pte Ltd

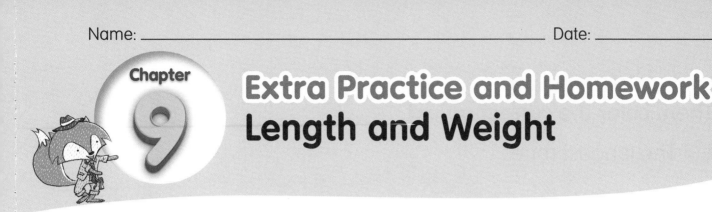

Chapter 9

Extra Practice and Homework
Length and Weight

Activity 2   Comparing More Lengths

Look at the picture.
Then, fill in each blank with the correct name.

1

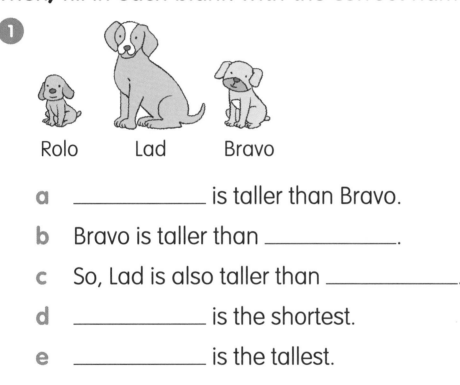

Rolo   Lad   Bravo

a   _____ is taller than Bravo.

b   Bravo is taller than _____.

c   So, Lad is also taller than _____.

d   _____ is the shortest.

e   _____ is the tallest.

Read.
Then, draw the tails on the mouse and the dog.

2 The mouse has a longer tail than the cat.
The cat has a longer tail than the dog.
So, the mouse has a longer tail than the dog.

© 2020 Marshall Cavendish Education Pte Ltd

Look at each picture.
Then, color the correct object.

3 The longest rope

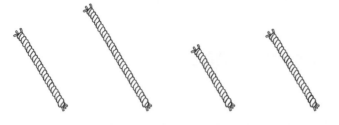

4 The shortest vegetable

5 The girl with the longest hair

6 The tallest animal

© 2020 Marshall Cavendish Education Pte Ltd

Look at the picture.
Then, fill in each blank with "taller," "tallest," "shorter," or "shortest."

7 ostrich   elephant   giraffe

rabbit

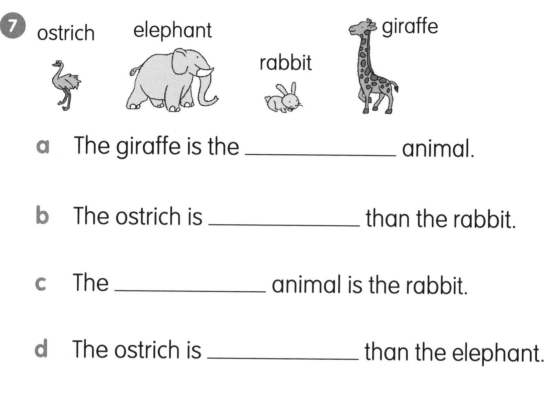

a   The giraffe is the _____ animal.

b   The ostrich is _____ than the rabbit.

c   The _____ animal is the rabbit.

d   The ostrich is _____ than the elephant.

Look at the picture.
Then, fill in each blank with A, B, or C.

8 Wire A

Wire B

Wire C

a   Wire _____ is longer than Wire B.

b   Wire B is longer than Wire _____.

c   Wire _____ is the longest wire.

© 2020 Marshall Cavendish Education Pte Ltd

9 The shelves hold Jake's and his sister's toys.

Find Jake's toys.
Use the clues below to help you.

Clues:
- Jake's toy is taller than the teddy bear.
- Jake has the longest toy.

Circle Jake's toys.

© 2020 Marshall Cavendish Education Pte Ltd

Extra Practice and Homework Grade 1B

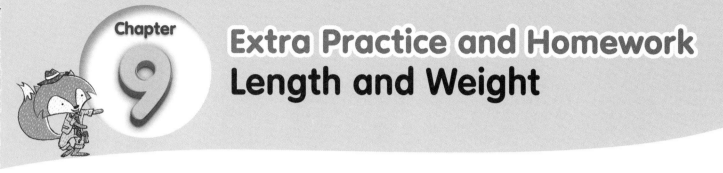

Chapter 9

Extra Practice and Homework
Length and Weight

Activity 3   Using a Start Line

Cut out the caterpillars.
Paste them on the box in the order shown.

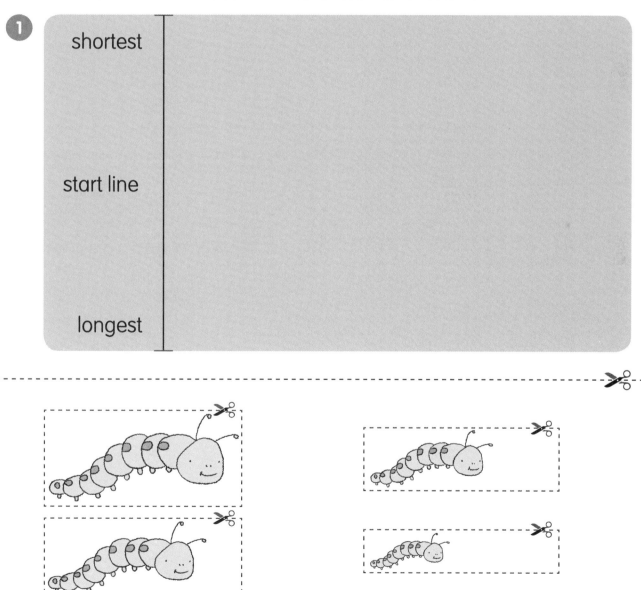

© 2020 Marshall Cavendish Education Pte Ltd

BLANK

© 2020 Marshall Cavendish Education Pte Ltd

Look at the pencil.
Draw a longer pencil.
Color it blue.
Draw a shorter pencil.
Color it green.

2

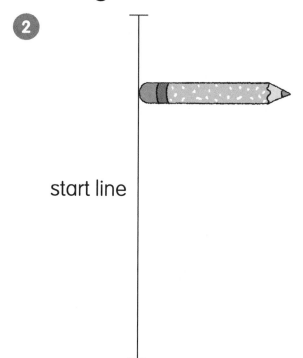

start line

Look at the bottle.
Draw a taller bottle.
Color it yellow.
Draw a shorter bottle.
Color it red.

3

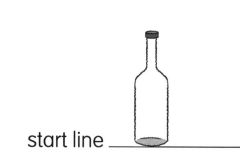

start line

© 2020 Marshall Cavendish Education Pte Ltd

4

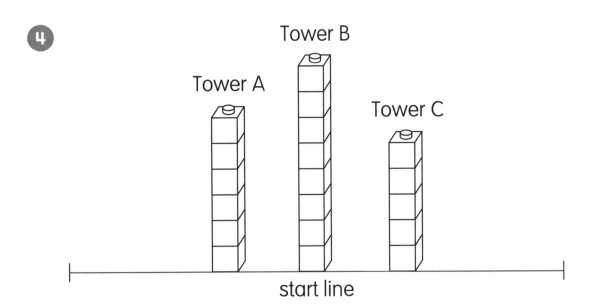

Tower B

Tower A

Tower C

start line

a   Draw a tower that is taller than Tower A but shorter than Tower B. Label it Tower D.

b   Draw another tower that is shorter than Tower C. Label it Tower E.

c   Color the tallest tower blue.

d   Color the shortest tower red.

© 2020 Marshall Cavendish Education Pte Ltd

Cut out the train parts.
Paste them below to make three trains of different lengths.

5

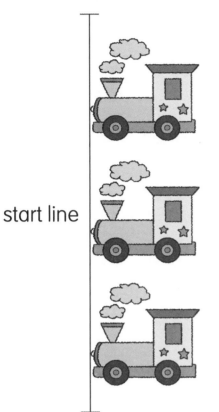

start line

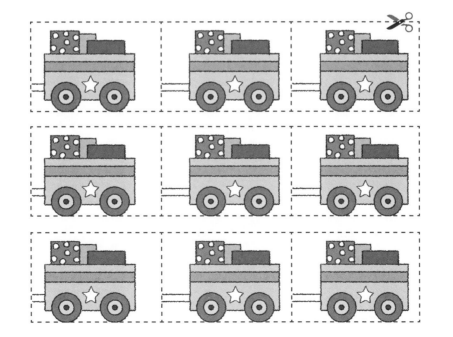

© 2020 Marshall Cavendish Education Pte Ltd

BLANK

© 2020 Marshall Cavendish Education Pte Ltd

Cut out the buildings.
Arrange and paste them below in the order shown.

6

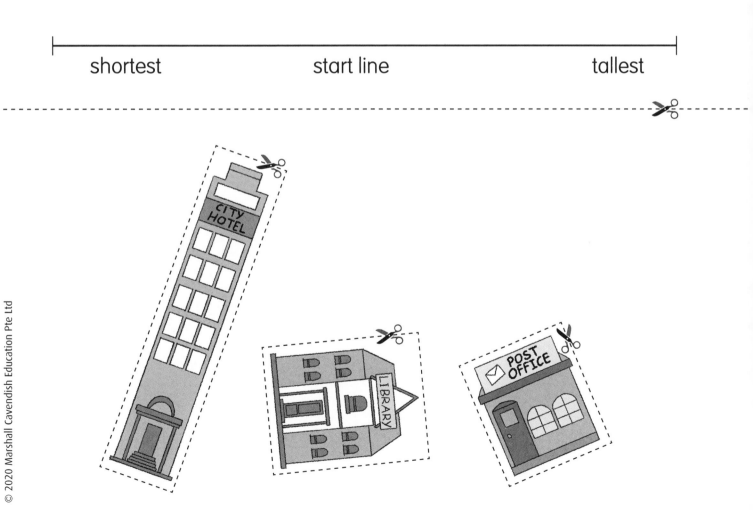

shortest   start line   tallest

CITY HOTEL

LIBRARY

POST OFFICE

© 2020 Marshall Cavendish Education Pte Ltd

BLANK

© 2020 Marshall Cavendish Education Pte Ltd

Activity 4   Measuring Lengths

Look at each picture.
Then, fill in each blank.

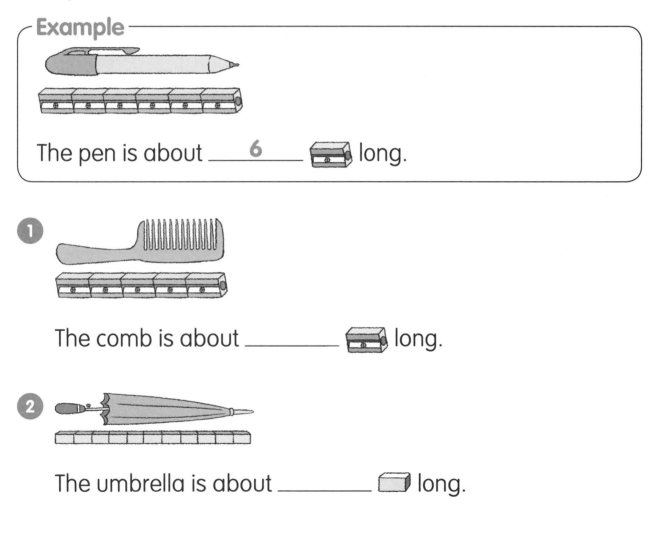

Example

The pen is about _____6_____ 🎁 long.

1

The comb is about _____ 🎁 long.

2

The umbrella is about _____ ▭ long.

© 2020 Marshall Cavendish Education Pte Ltd

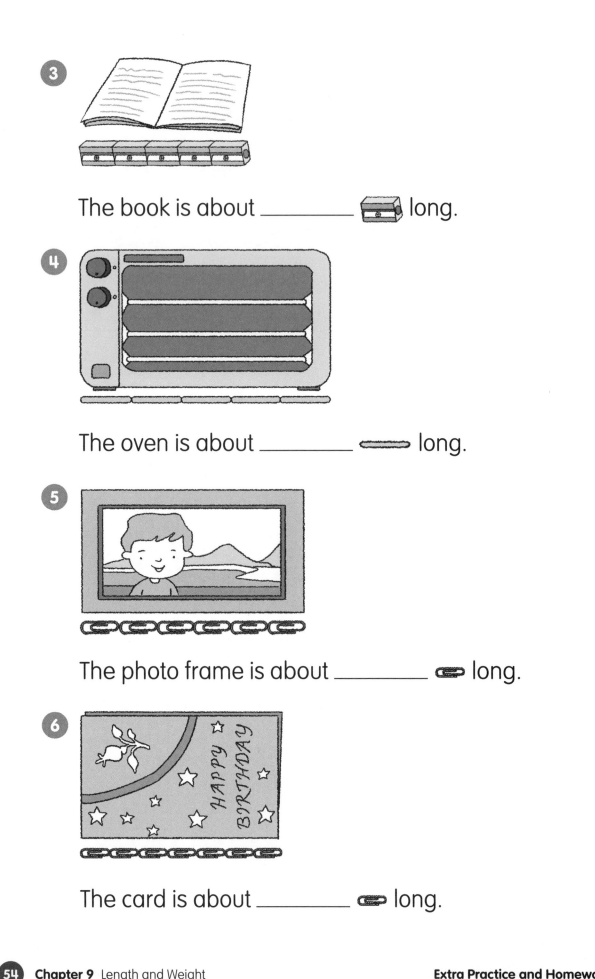

3

The book is about _____ 🗄 long.

4

The oven is about _____ ▭ long.

5

The photo frame is about _____ 🔗 long.

6

The card is about _____ 🔗 long.

© 2020 Marshall Cavendish Education Pte Ltd

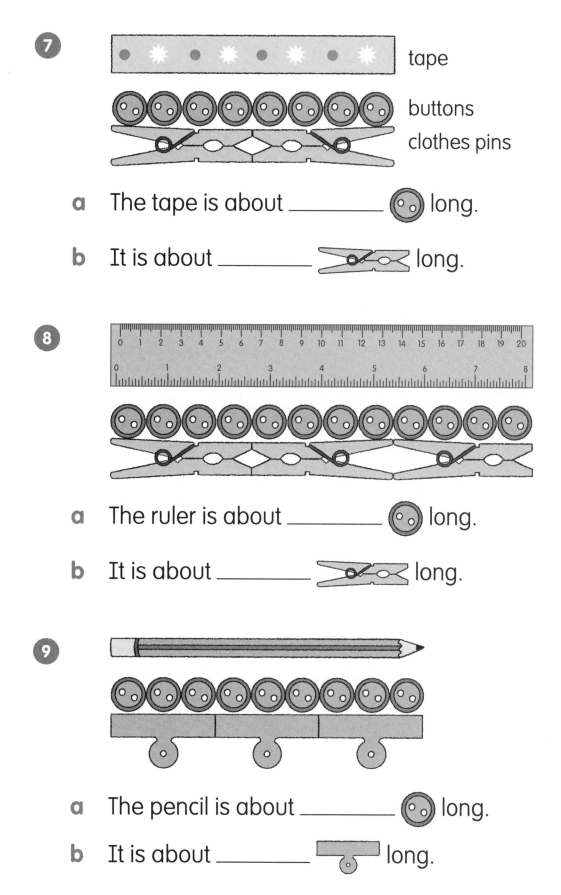

7

tape

buttons

clothes pins

a The tape is about _____ 🔘 long.

b It is about _____ ⬫ long.

8

a The ruler is about _____ 🔘 long.

b It is about _____ ⬫ long.

9

a The pencil is about _____ 🔘 long.

b It is about _____ long.

© 2020 Marshall Cavendish Education Pte Ltd

10

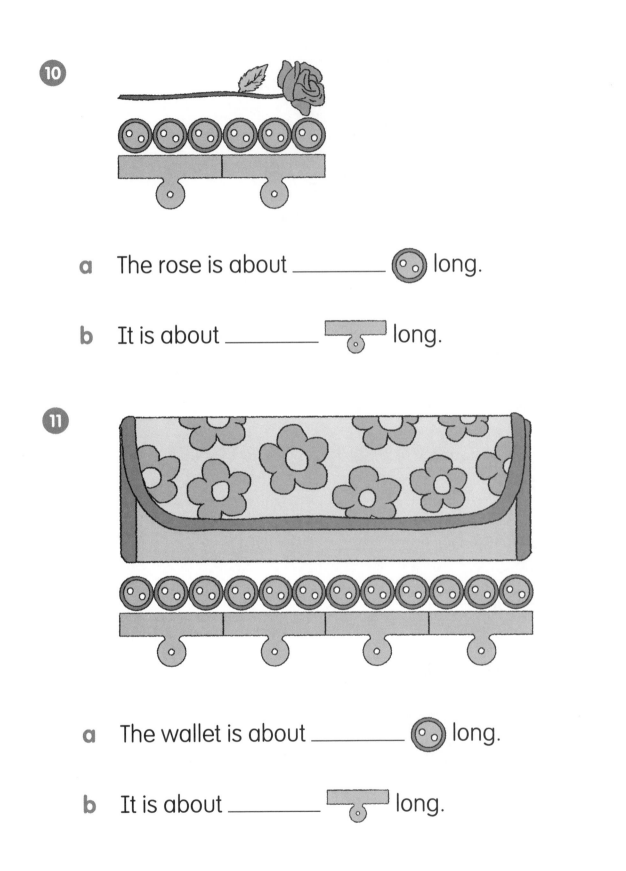

a The rose is about _____ 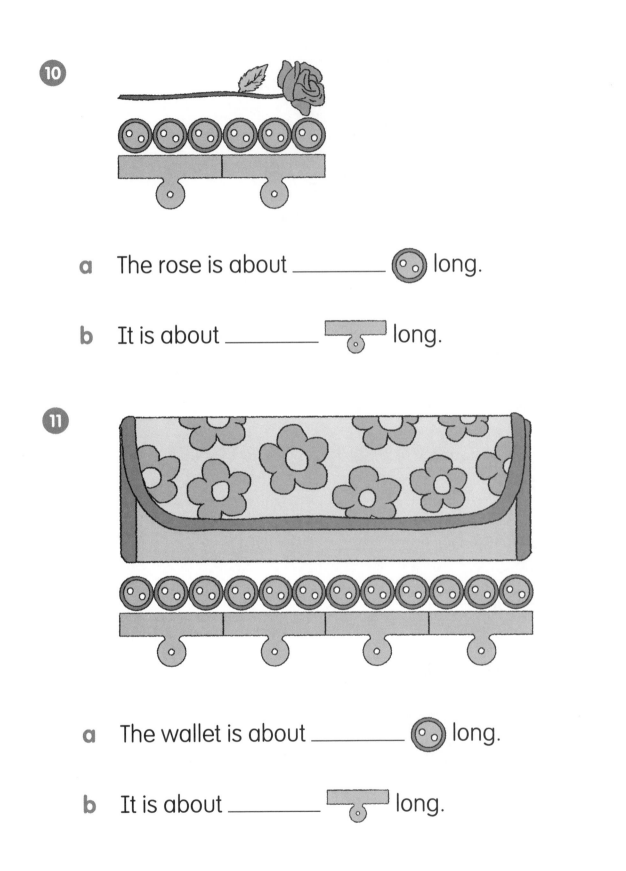 long.

b It is about _____ long.

11

a The wallet is about _____ long.

b It is about _____ long.

© 2020 Marshall Cavendish Education Pte Ltd

Chapter 9 Extra Practice and Homework
Length and Weight

Activity 5 Measuring Length in Units

Look at each picture.
Then, fill in each blank.

1 Each  stands for 1 unit.

The spoon is about _____ units long.

2 Each ⬓ stands for 1 unit.

The book is about _____ units long.

3 Each ⚾ stands for 1 unit.

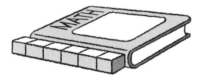

The bat is about _____ units long.

© 2020 Marshall Cavendish Education Pte Ltd

Look at the picture.
Then, fill in each blank.
Each [_____] **stands for 1 unit.**

4

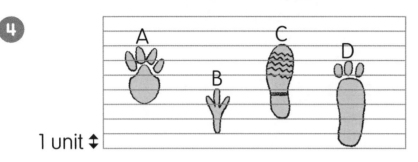

1 unit ↕

a   Footprint A is _____ units long.

b   Footprint B is _____ units long.

c   Footprint C is _____ units long.

d   Footprint D is _____ units long.

e   Footprint _____ is the longest.

f   Footprint _____ is shorter than Footprint A.

g   Which is longer, Footprint C or Footprint D? _____
     How much longer? _____ unit

h   Which is shorter, Footprint B or Footprint C? _____
     How much shorter? _____ units

© 2020 Marshall Cavendish Education Pte Ltd

Look at the picture.
Then, fill in each blank.
Each ☐ **stands for 1 unit.**

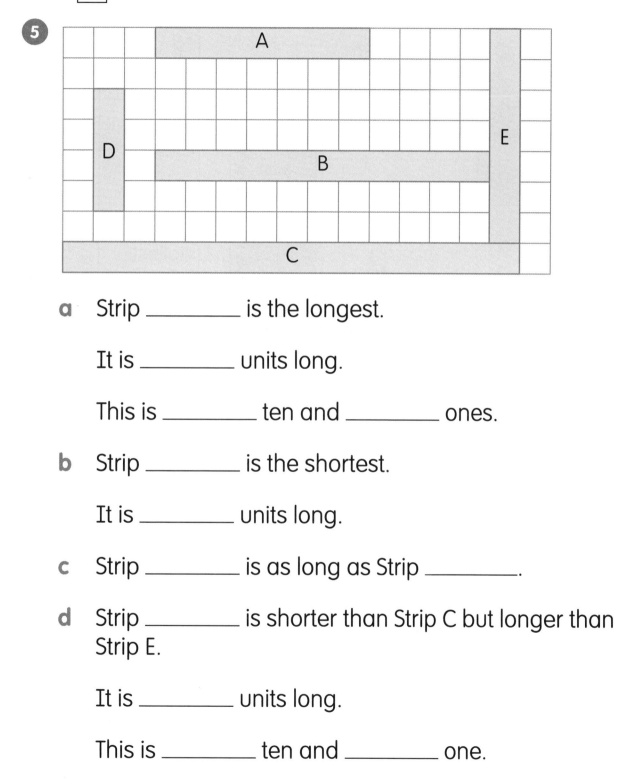

a Strip _____ is the longest.

It is _____ units long.

This is _____ ten and _____ ones.

b Strip _____ is the shortest.

It is _____ units long.

c Strip _____ is as long as Strip _____.

d Strip _____ is shorter than Strip C but longer than Strip E.

It is _____ units long.

This is _____ ten and _____ one.

© 2020 Marshall Cavendish Education Pte Ltd

Look at the picture.
Then, fill in each blank.
Each ☐ stands for 1 unit.

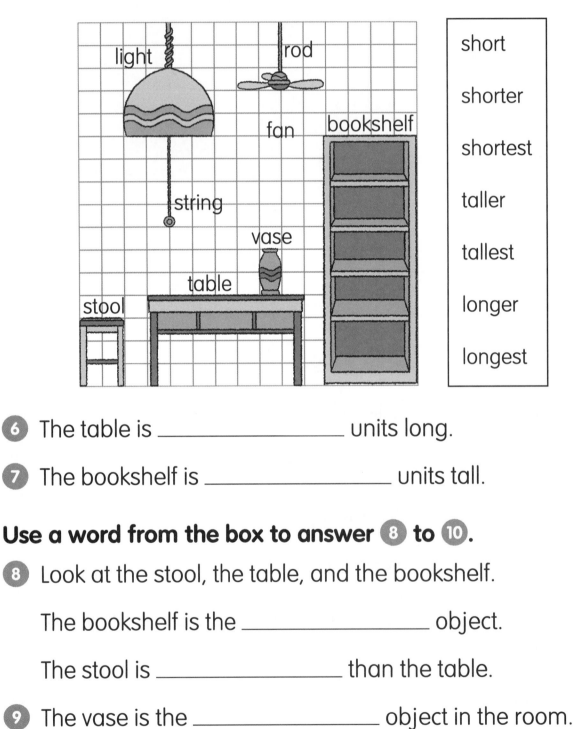

short

shorter

shortest

taller

tallest

longer

longest

6 The table is _____ units long.

7 The bookshelf is _____ units tall.

Use a word from the box to answer **8** to **10**.

8 Look at the stool, the table, and the bookshelf.

The bookshelf is the _____ object.

The stool is _____ than the table.

9 The vase is the _____ object in the room.

10 The string from the light is _____ than the rod of the fan.

© 2020 Marshall Cavendish Education Pte Ltd

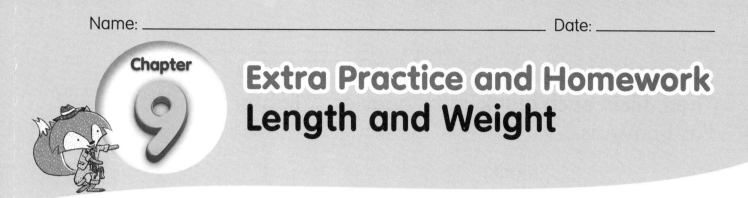

Chapter 9

Extra Practice and Homework
Length and Weight

Activity 6 Comparing Weights

Look at each picture.
Then, circle the answer.

1 Who is heavier?

James   John

2 Which is heavier?

crab

cat

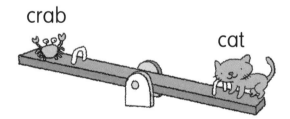

3 Which is lighter?

watermelon

lemon

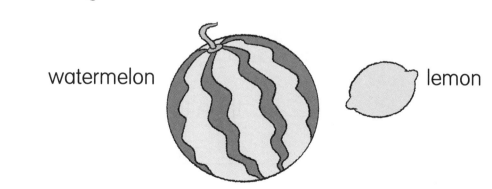

© 2020 Marshall Cavendish Education Pte Ltd

Look at each picture.
Then, fill in each blank with "heavier," "lighter," or
"as heavy as."

4

muffin
loaf of bread

The loaf of bread is _____ than the muffin.

5

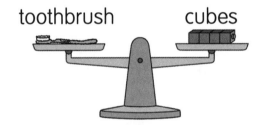

toothbrush
cubes

a The toothbrush is _____ the cubes.

b The cubes are _____ the toothbrush.

6

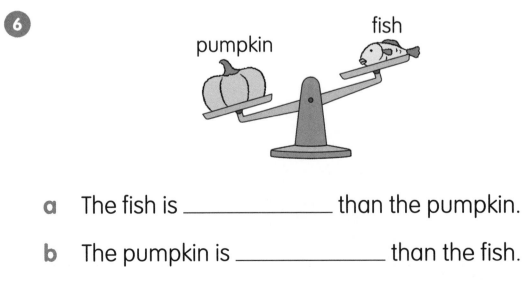

pumpkin
fish

a The fish is _____ than the pumpkin.

b The pumpkin is _____ than the fish.

© 2020 Marshall Cavendish Education Pte Ltd

Look at each picture.
Then, answer each question.

7

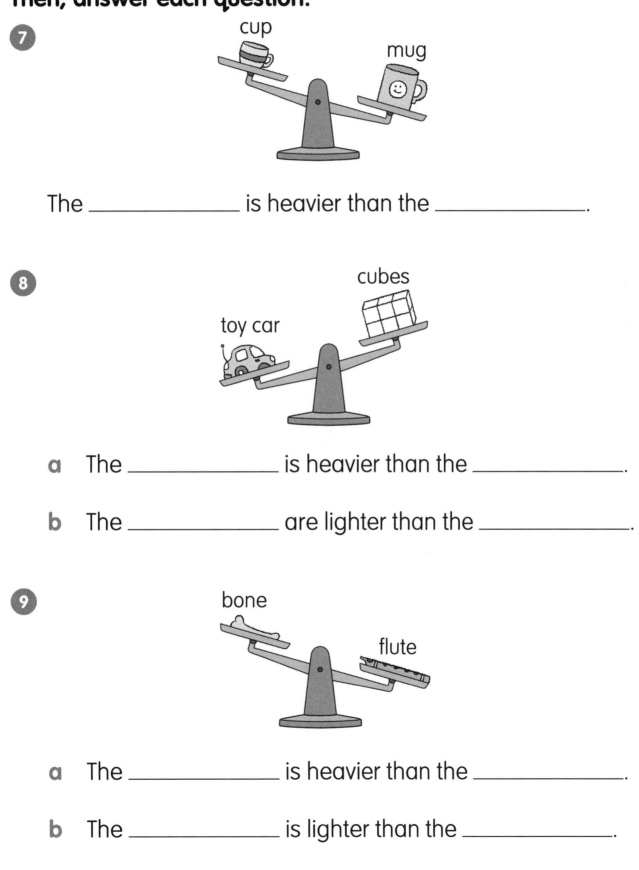

cup

mug

The _____ is heavier than the _____.

8

cubes

toy car

a The _____ is heavier than the _____.

b The _____ are lighter than the _____.

9

bone

flute

a The _____ is heavier than the _____.

b The _____ is lighter than the _____.

© 2020 Marshall Cavendish Education Pte Ltd

10 Mrs. Turner has an apple and an orange.

She puts them on a .
The orange is heavier than the apple.

apple

orange

Draw the apple and orange on the correct pans.

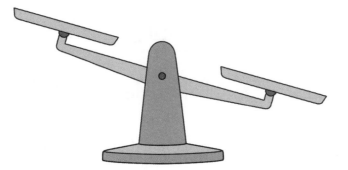

© 2020 Marshall Cavendish Education Pte Ltd

Guess which is heavier.

Circle the heavier object.

Then, check using a ⚖ **.**

Circle the heavier object.

11 a

My guess		The heavier object is	
orange	eraser	orange	eraser
book	a piece of paper	book	a piece of paper
a piece of paper	eraser	a piece of paper	eraser
orange	book	orange	book

Fill in the blank.

b   How many correct guesses did you make? _____

© 2020 Marshall Cavendish Education Pte Ltd

Look at each picture.
Then, fill in each blank.

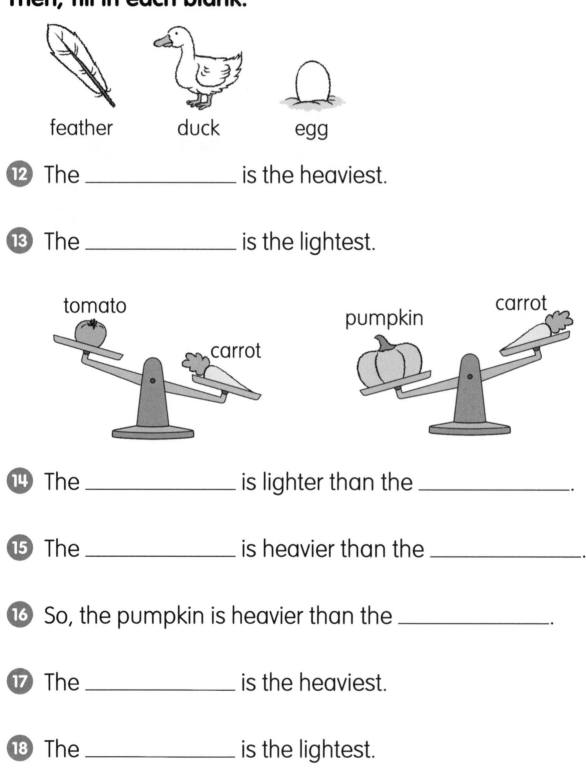

feather   duck   egg

12 The _____ is the heaviest.

13 The _____ is the lightest.

tomato   pumpkin   carrot

carrot

14 The _____ is lighter than the _____.

15 The _____ is heavier than the _____.

16 So, the pumpkin is heavier than the _____.

17 The _____ is the heaviest.

18 The _____ is the lightest.

© 2020 Marshall Cavendish Education Pte Ltd

Chapter 9

Extra Practice and Homework
Length and Weight

Activity 7   Measuring Weight

Look at each picture.
Then, fill in each blank.

1

paper ball

clothes pins

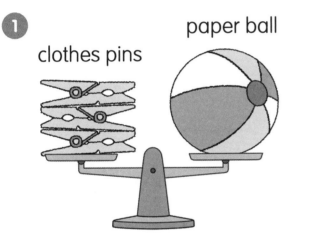

The weight of the paper ball is about _____ .

2 doll

toy bricks

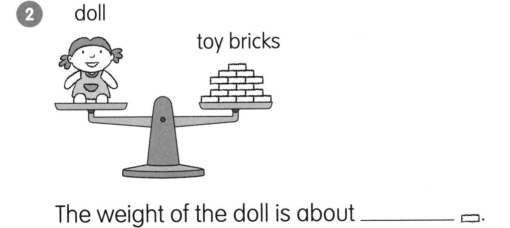

The weight of the doll is about _____ ⌑.

© 2020 Marshall Cavendish Education Pte Ltd

3 toy hippo

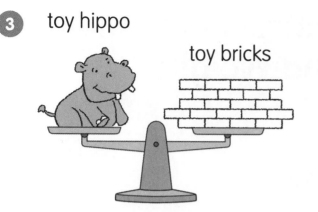

toy bricks

The weight of the toy hippo is about _____ 🔳.

4 toy cat

toy bricks

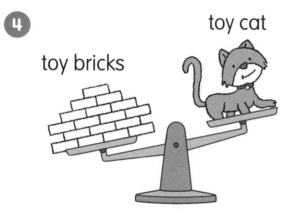

The weight of the toy cat is more than 15 toy bricks.

The weight of the toy cat is about _____ 🔳.

© 2020 Marshall Cavendish Education Pte Ltd

Look at the picture.
Then, fill in each blank.

5

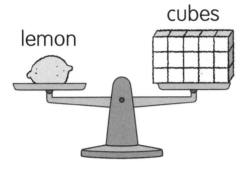 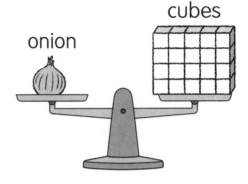

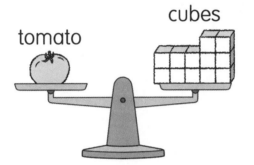

a The weight of the tomato is about _____ ⬜.

b The weight of the lemon is about _____ ⬦.

c The weight of the onion is about _____ ⬦.

d The lemon is heavier than the _____.

e The lemon is lighter than the _____.

f The _____ is the heaviest.

g The _____ is the lightest.

h Order the objects from lightest to heaviest.

_____ , _____ , _____
    lightest   heaviest

© 2020 Marshall Cavendish Education Pte Ltd

Look at the picture.
Then, fill in each blank.

6

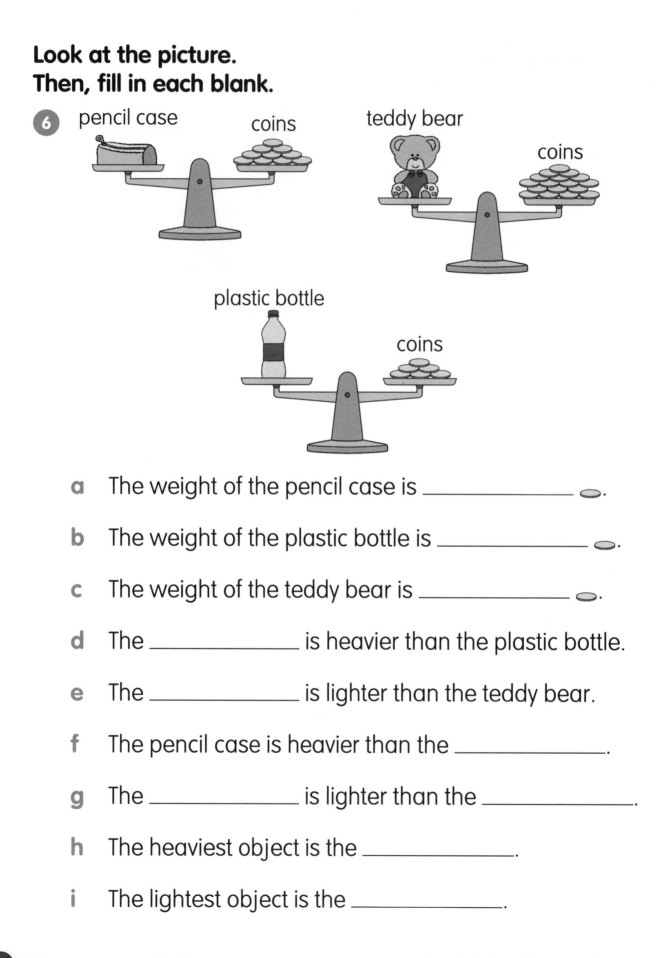

pencil case   coins   teddy bear   coins   plastic bottle   coins

a   The weight of the pencil case is _____ ⬭.

b   The weight of the plastic bottle is _____ ⬭.

c   The weight of the teddy bear is _____ ⬭.

d   The _____ is heavier than the plastic bottle.

e   The _____ is lighter than the teddy bear.

f   The pencil case is heavier than the _____.

g   The _____ is lighter than the _____.

h   The heaviest object is the _____.

i   The lightest object is the _____.

© 2020 Marshall Cavendish Education Pte Ltd

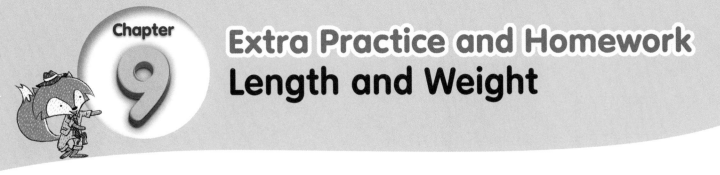

Chapter 9
Extra Practice and Homework
Length and Weight

Activity 8   Measuring Weight in Units

Look at each picture.
Then, fill in each blank.

1 Each ⬭ stands for 1 unit.

vegetable chips

The weight of the bag of vegetable chips is about
_____ units.

2 Each ⬚ stands for 1 unit.

baby carrot

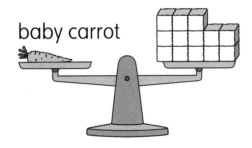

The weight of the baby carrot is about _____ units.

© 2020 Marshall Cavendish Education Pte Ltd

3 Each stands for 1 unit.

present

The weight of the present is about _____ units.

4 Each ⬯ stands for 1 unit.

lemon

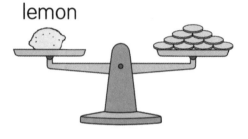

The weight of the lemon is about _____ units.

5 Each ▯ stands for 1 unit.

egg

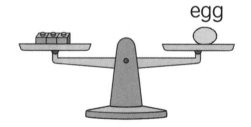

The weight of the egg is about _____ units.

6 Each ▭ stands for 1 unit.

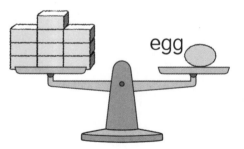

egg

The weight of the egg is about _____ units.

© 2020 Marshall Cavendish Education Pte Ltd

Look at the picture.
Then, fill in each blank.

7 Each 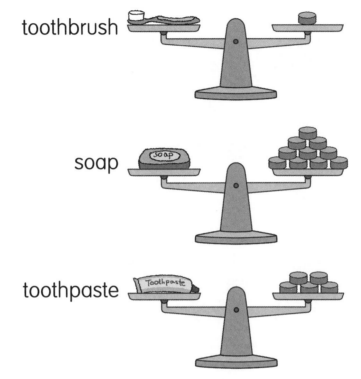 stands for 1 unit.

a The weight of the toothbrush is about _____ unit.

b The weight of the soap is about _____ units.

c The weight of the toothpaste is about _____ units.

d The _____ is lighter than the toothpaste.

e The soap is heavier than the _____.

f The _____ is the heaviest.

g The _____ is the lightest.

h Order the objects from lightest to heaviest.

_____, _____, _____
    lightest   heaviest

© 2020 Marshall Cavendish Education Pte Ltd

Look at the picture.
Then, fill in each blank.

8 Each ⬭ stands for 1 unit.

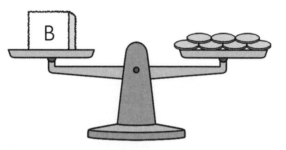

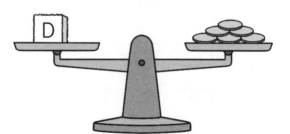

© 2020 Marshall Cavendish Education Pte Ltd

a The weight of Box A is about _____ units.

b The weight of Box B is about _____ units.

c The weight of Box C is about _____ units.

d The weight of Box D is about _____ units.

e Box _____ is the heaviest.

f Box _____ is the lightest.

g Box _____ is heavier than Box D.

h Box _____ is lighter than Box A.

9 Order the boxes from heaviest to lightest.

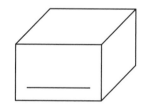 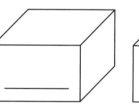 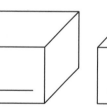 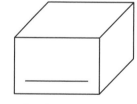

heaviest   lightest

© 2020 Marshall Cavendish Education Pte Ltd

Solve.

10 Three children bring their pets to an outing.
Ben's pet is heavier than Ally's pet.
Charlie's pet is lighter than Ben's pet.
Ally's pet is the lightest.

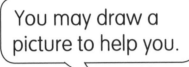
You may draw a picture to help you.

a Whose pet is the heaviest?

_____ pet is the heaviest.

b Whose pet is not the heaviest and not the lightest?

_____ pet is not the heaviest and not the lightest.

© 2020 Marshall Cavendish Education Pte Ltd

Name: _____ Date: _____

Mathematical Habit 6 Use precise mathematical language

Look around your classroom or school.
Find three objects.
Draw them in the space.

[drawing space]

Write three sentences about these objects.
Use three or more words from the box.

| longer | longest | shorter | shortest | taller |
| tallest | lighter | lightest | heavy | heaviest |

_____

_____

_____

_____

_____

_____

© 2020 Marshall Cavendish Education Pte Ltd

1 Mathematical Habit **2** Use mathematical reasoning

Look at the picture.

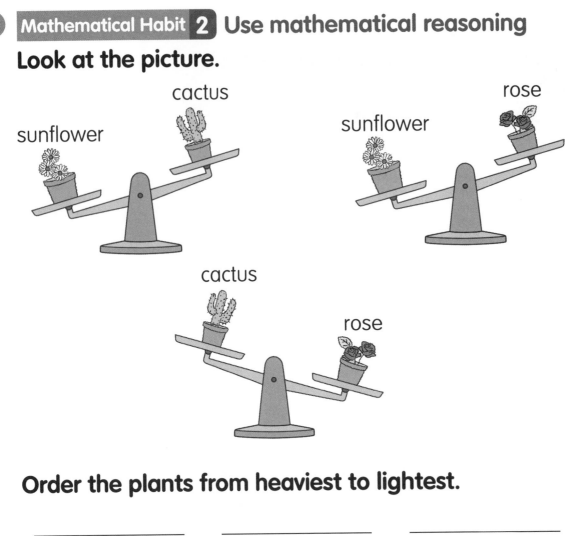

Order the plants from heaviest to lightest.

_____   _____   _____

heaviest   lightest

2 Mathematical Habit **7** Look for structure

Order the bears from tallest to shortest.
Write the correct letter on each blank.

_____   _____   _____

tallest   shortest

© 2020 Marshall Cavendish Education Pte Ltd

SCHOOL-to-HOME CONNECTIONS

Numbers to 120

Dear Family,

In this chapter, your child will work with numbers to 120. Skills your child will practice include:
- counting from 41 to 120
- reading and writing from 41 to 120 in numbers and in words
- using a place-value chart to show numbers to 100
- representing numbers to 100 as tens and ones
- comparing and ordering numbers to 100

Math Practice

At the end of this chapter, you may want to carry out this activity with your child. This activity will help to strengthen your child's number sense.

Activity 1

- Gather 120 plastic straws and 12 rubber bands.
- Scatter the straws on a flat surface and have your child make bundles of 10, using a rubber band to secure each bundle.
- Remove the rubber band from one bundle of 10 to make 'ones'.
- Select any number of bundles and any number of ones and ask your child to count, starting with groups of 10.
- Repeat the above step several times.

Math Talk

Scatter paper clips or other small identical objects on a flat surface. Ask your child to help you make groups of 10, calling them by name. Begin with **ten, twenty, thirty,** and continue through **one hundred and twenty**.

© 2020 Marshall Cavendish Education Pte Ltd

BLANK

Name: _____ Date: _____

Extra Practice and Homework
Numbers to 120

Activity 1   Counting to 120

Count on by tens and ones.
Write each missing number.

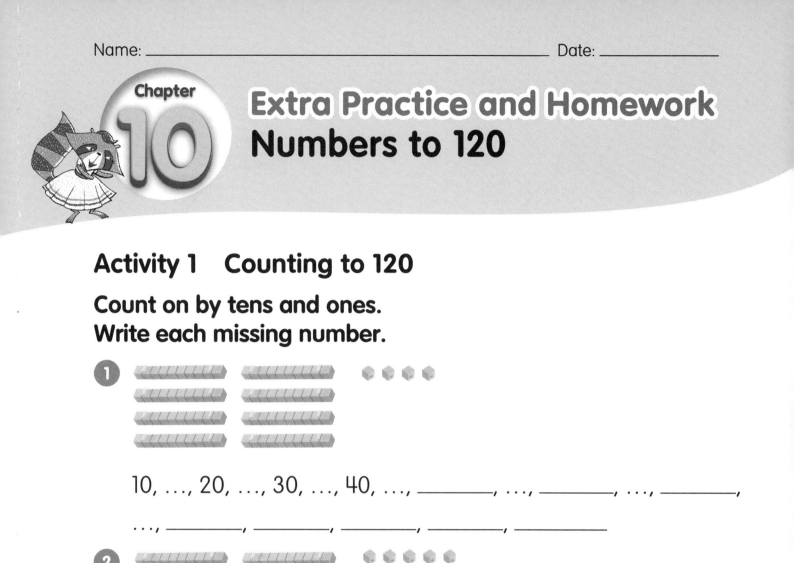

1

10, …, 20, …, 30, …, 40, …, _____, …, _____, …, _____,

…, _____, _____, _____, _____, _____

2

10, …, 20, …, 30, …, 40, …, _____, …, _____, _____,

_____, _____, _____, _____, _____,

_____, _____

3

10, …, 20, …, 30, …, 40, …, _____, …, _____, …,

_____, …, _____, …, _____, _____, _____

© 2020 Marshall Cavendish Education Pte Ltd

Write each number.

4 _____ sixty-eight

5 _____ eighty-four

Write each number in words.

6 **71**

_____

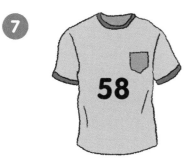

7 **58**

_____

8 **97**

_____

© 2020 Marshall Cavendish Education Pte Ltd

Guess the number of 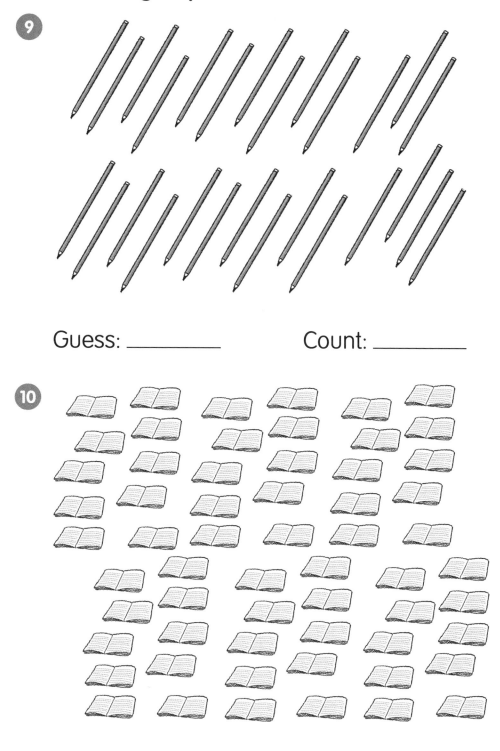 **and** 📖 **.**

Then, circle groups of 10 and count on.

9

Guess: _____   Count: _____

10

Guess: _____   Count: _____

© 2020 Marshall Cavendish Education Pte Ltd

Count on by tens and ones.
Then, write each number and word.

		Number	Word
11	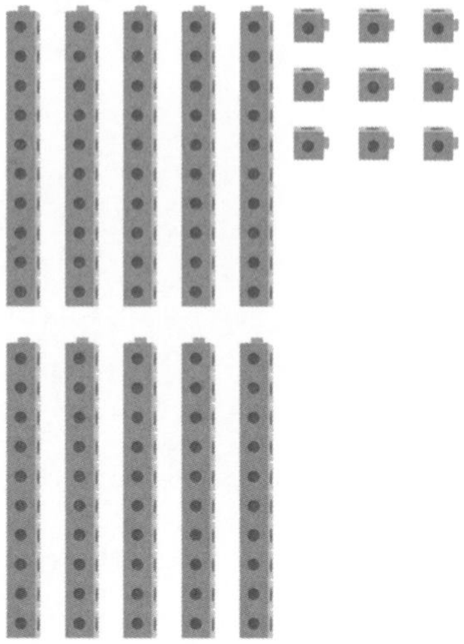		
12	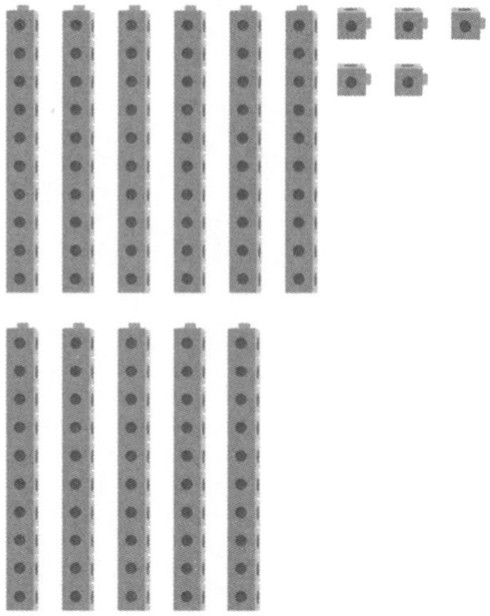		
13	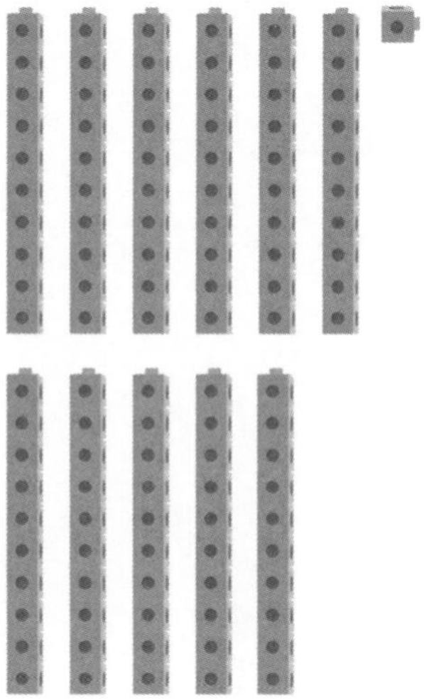		

© 2020 Marshall Cavendish Education Pte Ltd

Roy Rodent is finding its way to the yummy cheese.
Help him by drawing a path from 40 to 120.
Count on by tens.

14

Start

40	41	42	43	45	46	47	48
49	50	51	67	68	69	79	89
59	60	52	53	54	55	56	99
112	61	70	71	72	73	57	58
113	62	78	80	90	74	75	108
114	63	88	81	91	100	76	77
115	64	98	82	92	101	110	78
116	65	118	83	93	102	111	120

cheese

© 2020 Marshall Cavendish Education Pte Ltd

Count and write from 1 to 120.

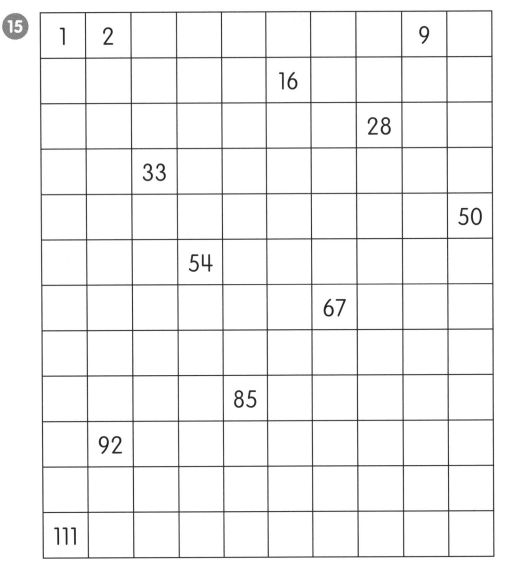

15

1	2							9	
				16					
						28			
	33								
									50
		54							
				67					
		85							
92									
111									

Count and color the numbers in **15**.

16 Count on from 1 to 120 by tens.
Color these boxes green.

17 Count on from 101 to 109 by ones.
Color these boxes blue.

© 2020 Marshall Cavendish Education Pte Ltd

Chapter 10 Extra Practice and Homework
Numbers to 120

Activity 2 Place Value

Fill in each blank.

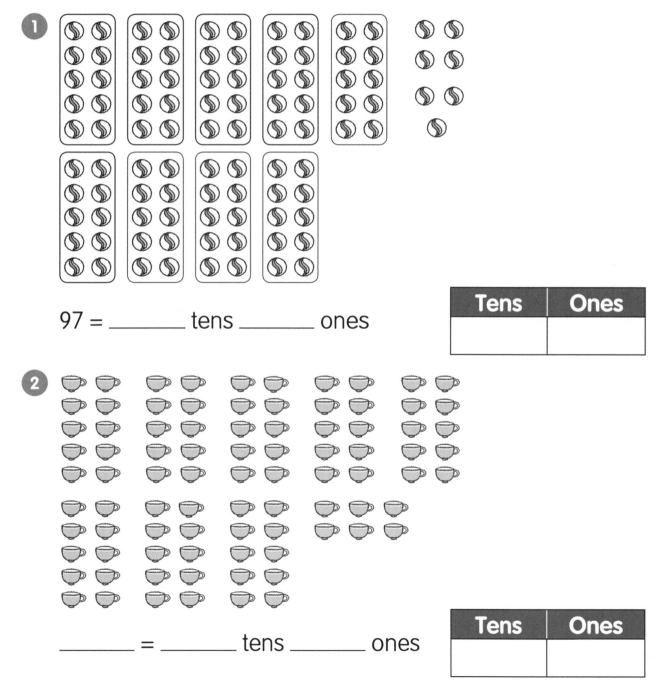

1

97 = _____ tens _____ ones

Tens	Ones

2

_____ = _____ tens _____ ones

Tens	Ones

© 2020 Marshall Cavendish Education Pte Ltd

Juan wants to show 104 in two different ways.
Draw [‏‏‎ ‎] **for tens and** ☐ **for ones to show the correct answer.**

③

Example	Way 1	Way 2
[‏‏‎ ‎] ☐ [‏‏‎ ‎] ☐ [‏‏‎ ‎] ☐ [‏‏‎ ‎] ☐ [‏‏‎ ‎] [‏‏‎ ‎] [‏‏‎ ‎] [‏‏‎ ‎] [‏‏‎ ‎] [‏‏‎ ‎]		

He also wants to show 85 in two different ways.
Draw [‏‏‎ ‎] **for tens and** ☐ **for ones to show the correct answer.**

④

1st way	2nd way

© 2020 Marshall Cavendish Education Pte Ltd

Color the balloons that show each number correctly.

5 83

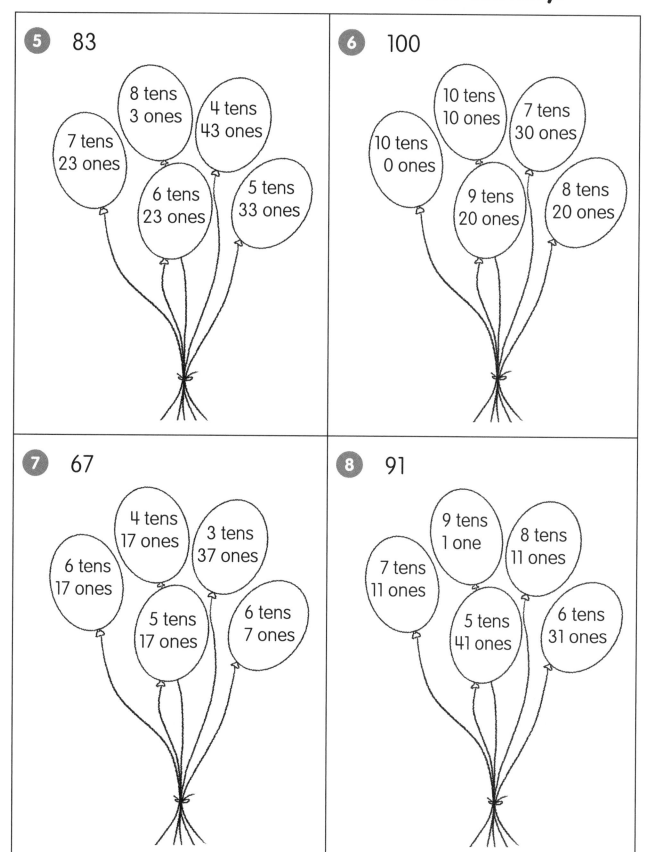

- 7 tens 23 ones
- 8 tens 3 ones
- 4 tens 43 ones
- 6 tens 23 ones
- 5 tens 33 ones

6 100

- 10 tens 0 ones
- 10 tens 10 ones
- 7 tens 30 ones
- 9 tens 20 ones
- 8 tens 20 ones

7 67

- 6 tens 17 ones
- 4 tens 17 ones
- 3 tens 37 ones
- 5 tens 17 ones
- 6 tens 7 ones

8 91

- 7 tens 11 ones
- 9 tens 1 one
- 8 tens 11 ones
- 5 tens 41 ones
- 6 tens 31 ones

© 2020 Marshall Cavendish Education Pte Ltd

Use tens and ones to write each number in different ways.

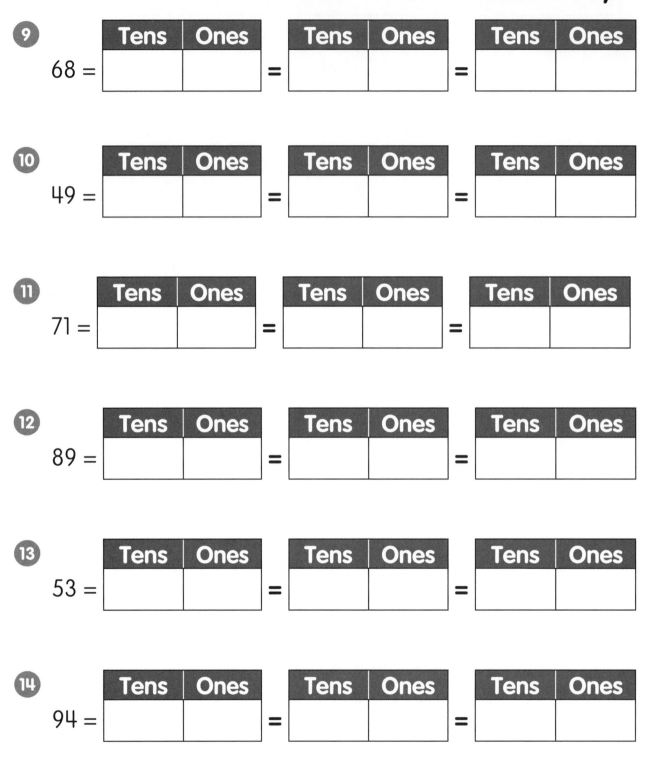

9

68 = | Tens | Ones |
| --- | --- |
| | |

= | Tens | Ones |
| --- | --- |
| | |

= | Tens | Ones |
| --- | --- |
| | |

10

49 = | Tens | Ones |
| --- | --- |
| | |

= | Tens | Ones |
| --- | --- |
| | |

= | Tens | Ones |
| --- | --- |
| | |

11

71 = | Tens | Ones |
| --- | --- |
| | |

= | Tens | Ones |
| --- | --- |
| | |

= | Tens | Ones |
| --- | --- |
| | |

12

89 = | Tens | Ones |
| --- | --- |
| | |

= | Tens | Ones |
| --- | --- |
| | |

= | Tens | Ones |
| --- | --- |
| | |

13

53 = | Tens | Ones |
| --- | --- |
| | |

= | Tens | Ones |
| --- | --- |
| | |

= | Tens | Ones |
| --- | --- |
| | |

14

94 = | Tens | Ones |
| --- | --- |
| | |

= | Tens | Ones |
| --- | --- |
| | |

= | Tens | Ones |
| --- | --- |
| | |

© 2020 Marshall Cavendish Education Pte Ltd

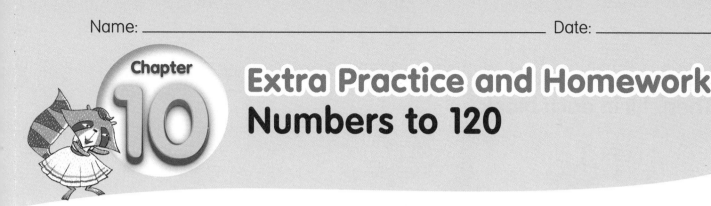

Chapter 10

Extra Practice and Homework
Numbers to 120

Activity 3 Comparing, Ordering, and Number Patterns

Fill in each blank.
Use the counting tape to help you.

75	76	77	78	79	80	81	82	83	84	85

1 2 more than 80 is _____.

2 2 less than 80 is _____.

3 _____ is 4 more than 79.

4 _____ is 3 less than 85.

Fill in each blank with >, <, or =.

5 50 ◯ 48

6 76 ◯ 78

7 63 ◯ 62

8 92 ◯ 89

9 59 ◯ 5 tens 7 ones

10 3 tens 16 ones ◯ 46

11 8 tens 16 ones ◯ 86

12 89 ◯ 8 tens 19 ones

13 63 ◯ 5 tens 13 ones

14 1 tens 12 ones ◯ 22

© 2020 Marshall Cavendish Education Pte Ltd

Compare the numbers.
Then, fill in each blank.

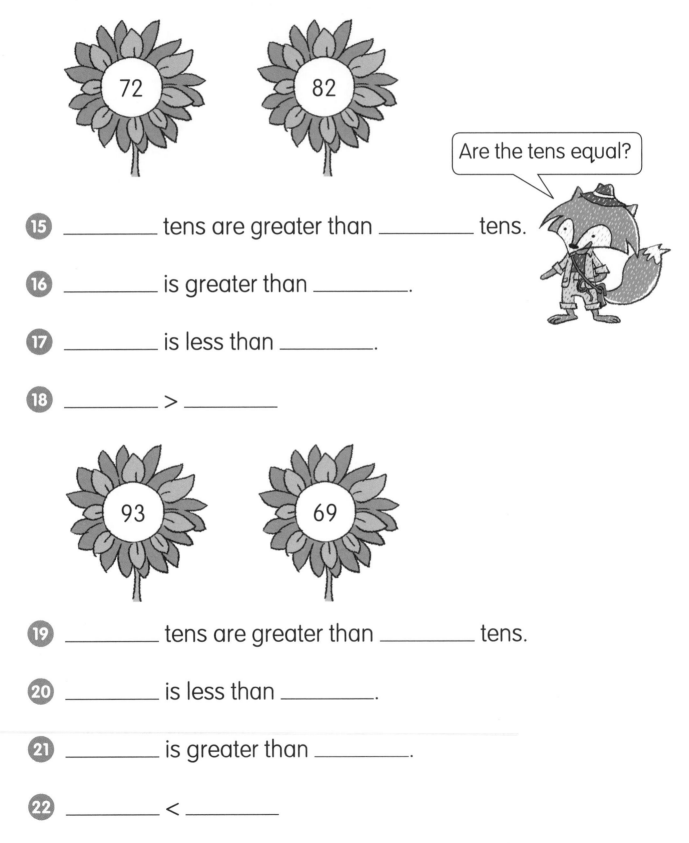

72   82

Are the tens equal?

15 _____ tens are greater than _____ tens.

16 _____ is greater than _____.

17 _____ is less than _____.

18 _____ > _____

93   69

19 _____ tens are greater than _____ tens.

20 _____ is less than _____.

21 _____ is greater than _____.

22 _____ < _____

© 2020 Marshall Cavendish Education Pte Ltd

Compare the numbers.
Then, fill in each blank.

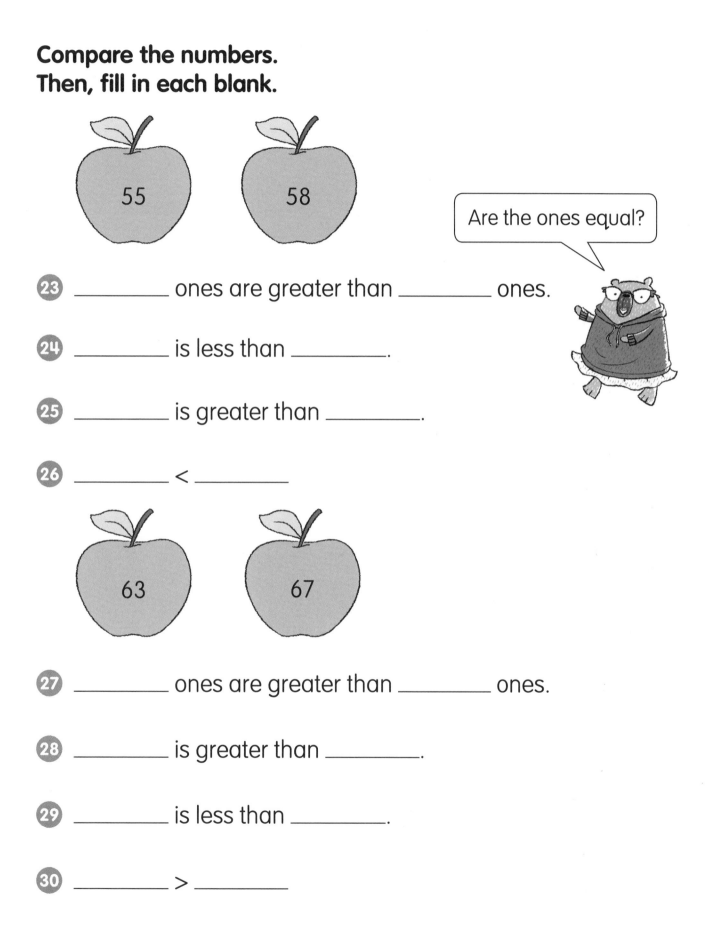

55   58

Are the ones equal?

23 _____ ones are greater than _____ ones.

24 _____ is less than _____ .

25 _____ is greater than _____ .

26 _____ < _____

63   67

27 _____ ones are greater than _____ ones.

28 _____ is greater than _____ .

29 _____ is less than _____ .

30 _____ > _____

© 2020 Marshall Cavendish Education Pte Ltd

Compare the numbers.
Then, fill in each blank.

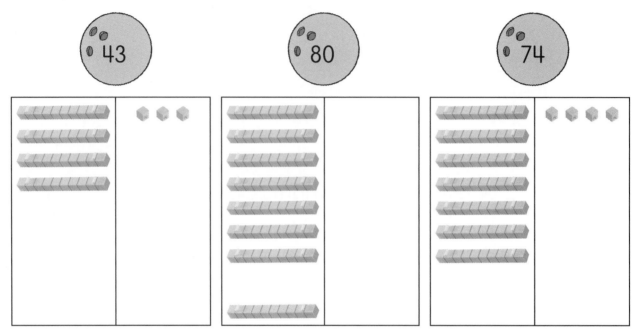

31 _____ is the greatest number.

32 _____ is the least number.

Compare and order the numbers.
Then, fill in each blank.

33 _____ is the least number.

34 _____ is the greatest number.

35 Order the numbers from least to greatest.

_____ , _____ , _____
    least   greatest

© 2020 Marshall Cavendish Education Pte Ltd

Ravi has ordered the numbers from greatest to least wrongly.

67   76   58
greatest   least

36 Help Ravi order the numbers correctly.

_____ , _____ , _____
greatest   least

The numbers are arranged in a pattern.
Write the missing numbers in each light bulb.
Then, write what the rule is.

37

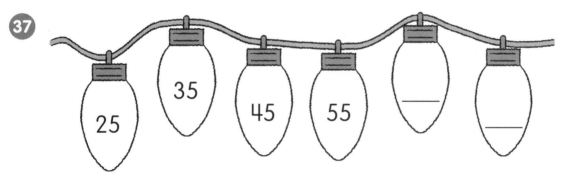

25   35   45   55   ___   ___

38 I find _____ more than a number by adding _____ to that number.

39 I find _____ less than a number by subtracting _____ from that number.

© 2020 Marshall Cavendish Education Pte Ltd

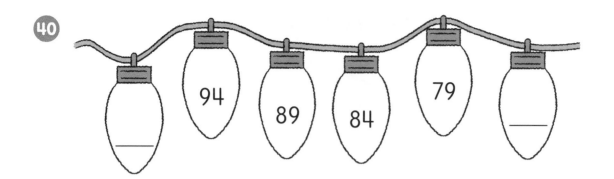

40

41 I find _____ less than a number by subtracting _____ from that number.

42 I find _____ more than a number by adding _____ to that number.

Write the missing numbers in each number pattern.

43

| 57 | 60 | 63 | 66 | _____ | _____ |

44

| _____ | 44 | 55 | 66 | 77 | _____ |

© 2020 Marshall Cavendish Education Pte Ltd

Mathematical Habit 7 **Make use of structure**

Pablo wants to create a number pattern.
Read the clues to help him.

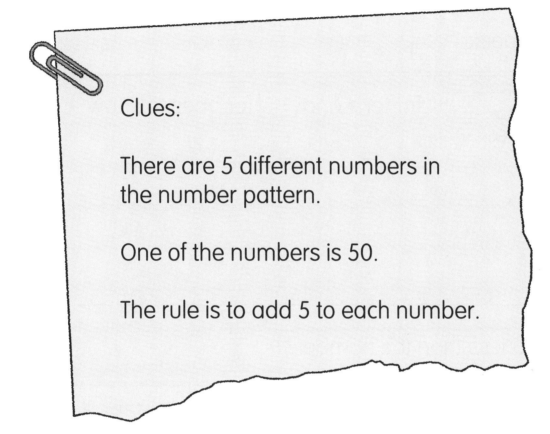

Clues:

There are 5 different numbers in
the number pattern.

One of the numbers is 50.

The rule is to add 5 to each number.

The number pattern is

1 Mathematical Habit **1** Persevere in solving problems

I am thinking of a number that is greater than 80 but less than 100.

The number is ☐.

Draw ☐ for tens and ☐ for ones to show the number.

What is 5 less than the number? ☐

What is 10 more than the number? ☐

2 Mathematical Habit **8** Look for patterns

Form a number pattern.

☐ ☐ 73 ☐ ☐

Write a rule for the number pattern.

_____

_____

© 2020 Marshall Cavendish Education Pte Ltd

Extra Practice and Homework Grade 1B

SCHOOL-to-HOME CONNECTIONS

Addition and Subtraction Within 100

Dear Family,

In this chapter, your child will add and subtract within 100. Skills your child will practice include:

- adding 2-digit and 1-digit numbers, with and without regrouping
- adding 2-digit and 2-digit numbers, with and without regrouping
- subtracting a 1-digit number from a 2-digit number, with and without regrouping
- subtracting a 2-digit number from a 2-digit number, with and without regrouping

Math Practice

At the end of this chapter, you may want to carry out these activities with your child. These activities will help to strengthen your child's understanding of addition and subtraction within 100. Take turns playing. Lead the first round to show your child how to play.

Math Talk

Ask your child to use toys or a handful of identical objects to demonstrate the meaning of **addition** and **subtraction**.

Activity 1

- Gather a pencil, a number cube, and a piece of paper.
- Roll the number cube twice to make a 2-digit number.
- Draw a number bond. Show the 2-digit number in tens and ones, and write the whole and parts in the number bond. For example, 51 can be written as shown.

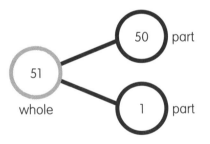

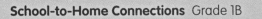

© 2020 Marshall Cavendish Education Pte Ltd

- Roll the number cube again to get a 1-digit number.
- Write an addition sentence to add the 2-digit and 1-digit numbers. For example, 51 + 3 = _____.
- Add the ones first. Then add the sum to the tens. For example, 1 + 3 = 4; 50 + 4 = 54; 51 + 3 = 54
- Have your child lead the next round.

Activity 2
- Gather a pencil, a number cube, and a piece of paper.
- Roll the number cube twice to make a 2-digit number.
- Draw a number bond. Show the 2-digit number in tens and ones, and write the whole and parts in the number bond. For example, 42 can be written as shown.

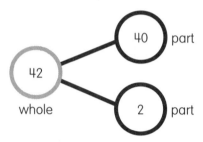

- Roll the number cube again to get a 1-digit number.
- Write a subtraction sentence to subtract the 1-digit number from the 2-digit number. For example, 42 – 6 = _____.
- Regroup the tens and ones.

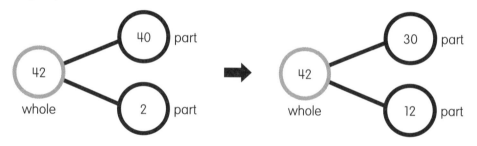

- Subtract. For example, 12 – 6 = 6; 30 + 6 = 36; 42 – 6 = 36.
- Have your child lead the next round.

© 2020 Marshall Cavendish Education Pte Ltd

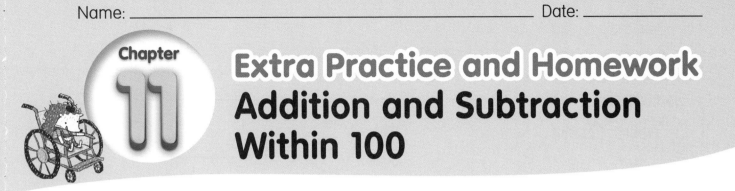

Chapter 11

Extra Practice and Homework
Addition and Subtraction Within 100

Activity 1   Addition Without Regrouping

Add.
Count on from the greater number.

Example

$52 + 3 =$ _____ **55**

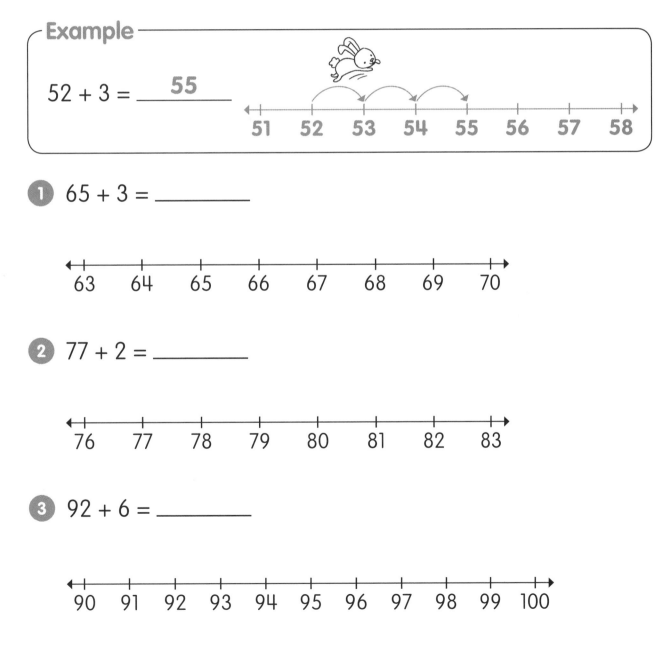

1   $65 + 3 =$ _____

2   $77 + 2 =$ _____

3   $92 + 6 =$ _____

© 2020 Marshall Cavendish Education Pte Ltd

Add.

© 2020 Marshall Cavendish Education Pte Ltd

Example

Tens	Ones
3	4
+	3
3	7

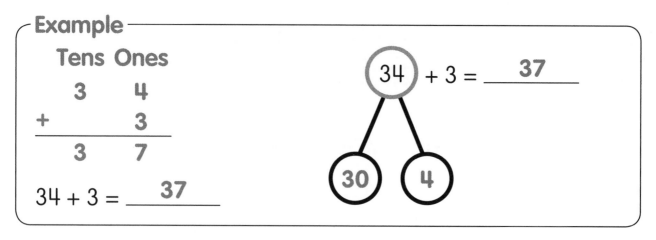

$34 + 3 = $ __37__

$34 + 3 = $ __37__

4

Tens	Ones
6	5
+	4

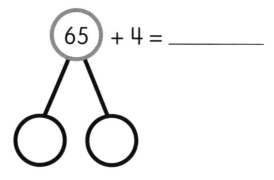

$65 + 4 = $ _____

$65 + 4 = $ _____

5

Tens	Ones
2	4
+	3

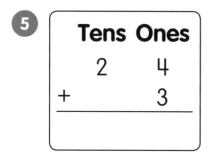

$24 + 3 = $ _____

$24 + 3 = $ _____

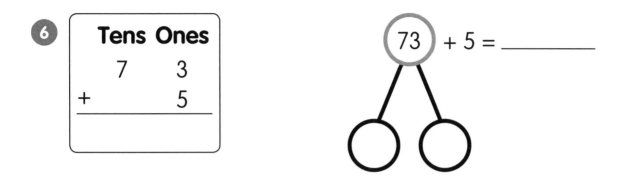

6

Tens	Ones
7	3
+	5

$73 + 5 = $ _____

$73 + 5 = $ _____

7

Tens	Ones
9	1
+	6

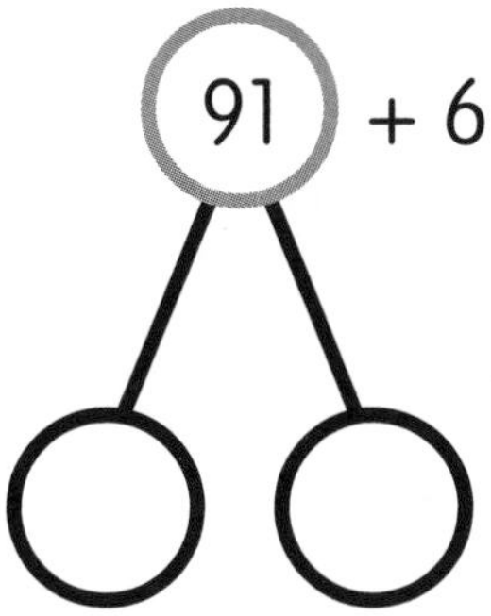

$91 + 6 = $ _____

$91 + 6 = $ _____

8

Tens	Ones
8	2
+	7

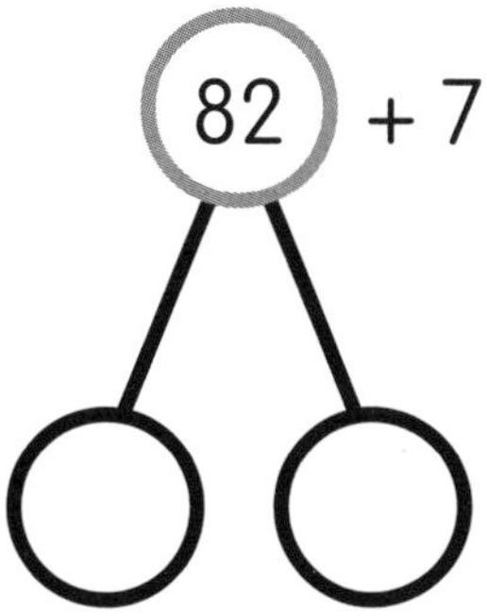

$82 + 7 = $ _____

$82 + 7 = $ _____

© 2020 Marshall Cavendish Education Pte Ltd

Count on by tens to add.
Then, fill in each blank.

Example

$41 + 20$

$= \underline{\ \ 61\ \ }$

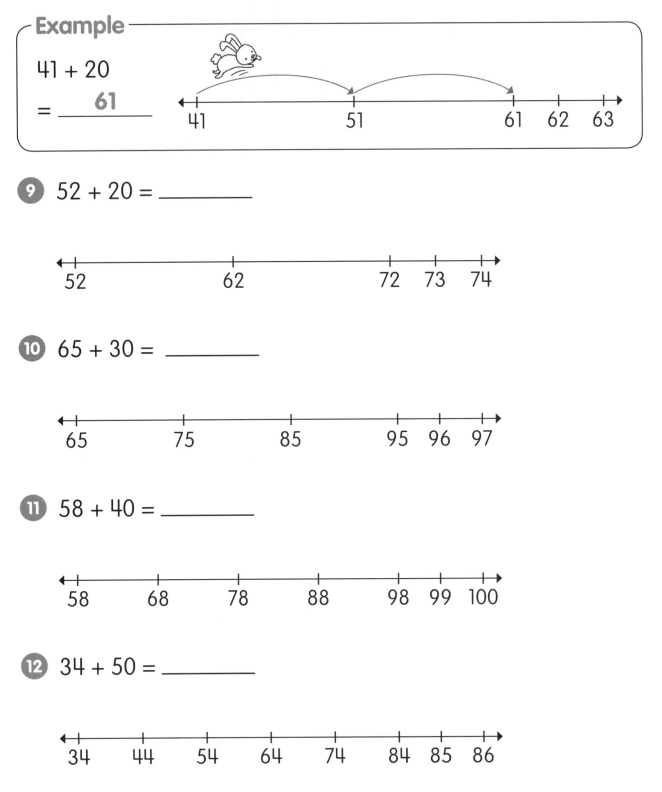

9 $52 + 20 = \underline{\hspace{2cm}}$

10 $65 + 30 = \underline{\hspace{2cm}}$

11 $58 + 40 = \underline{\hspace{2cm}}$

12 $34 + 50 = \underline{\hspace{2cm}}$

© 2020 Marshall Cavendish Education Pte Ltd

Add.

Example

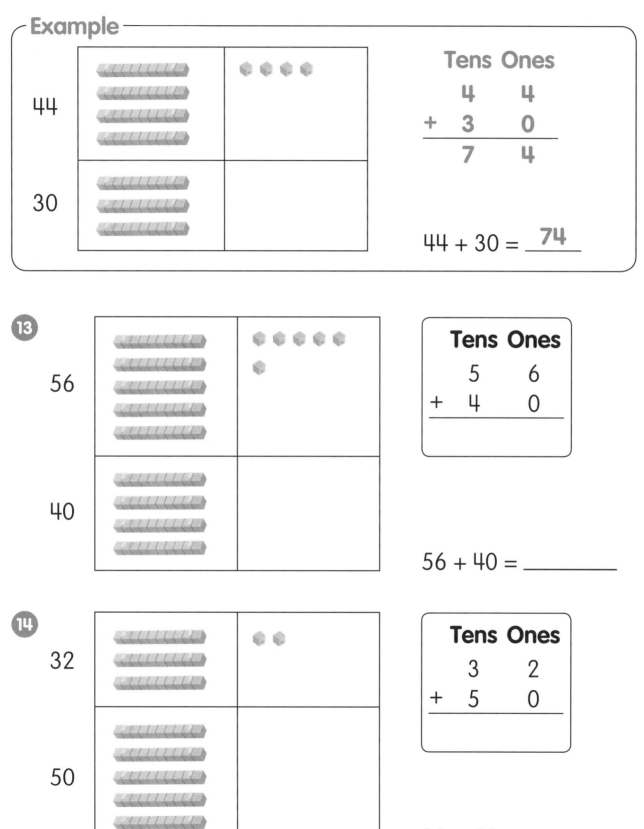

Tens Ones

$$
\begin{array}{cc}
 & 4 \quad 4 \\
+ & 3 \quad 0 \\
\hline
 & 7 \quad 4
\end{array}
$$

44 + 30 = __74__

13

56

40

Tens Ones

$$
\begin{array}{cc}
 & 5 \quad 6 \\
+ & 4 \quad 0 \\
\hline
\end{array}
$$

56 + 40 = _____

14

32

50

Tens Ones

$$
\begin{array}{cc}
 & 3 \quad 2 \\
+ & 5 \quad 0 \\
\hline
\end{array}
$$

32 + 50 = _____

© 2020 Marshall Cavendish Education Pte Ltd

1 Addition Without Regrouping

15

43

25

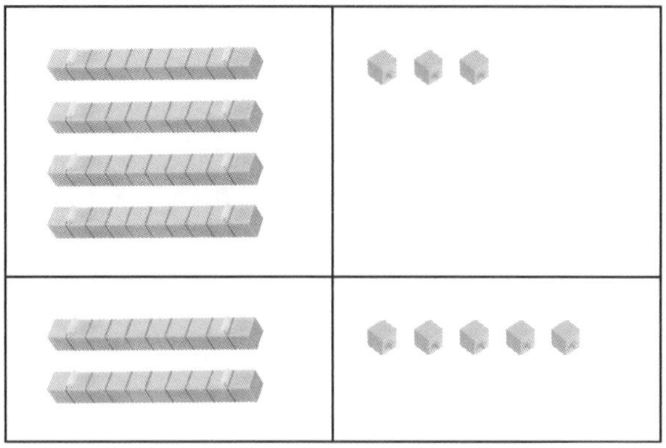

Tens	Ones
4	3
+ 2	5

$43 + 25 =$ _____

16

51

46

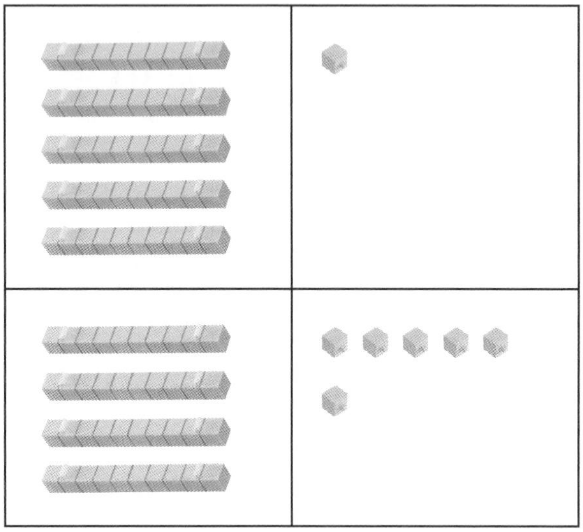

Tens	Ones
5	1
+ 4	6

$51 + 46 =$ _____

© 2020 Marshall Cavendish Education Pte Ltd

Jason is blowing bubbles.
Add to find the answers to burst the bubbles.

Example

```
  4   7
+ 2   1
─────────
  6   8
```

17

```
  5   0
+ 3   2
─────────
  □   □
```

18

```
  7   3
+ 1   5
─────────
  □   □
```

19

```
  9   5
+     4
─────────
  □   □
```

© 2020 Marshall Cavendish Education Pte Ltd

Pablo's race number is 87.
Which helmet matches his race number?
Add to find out.
Then, circle his helmet.

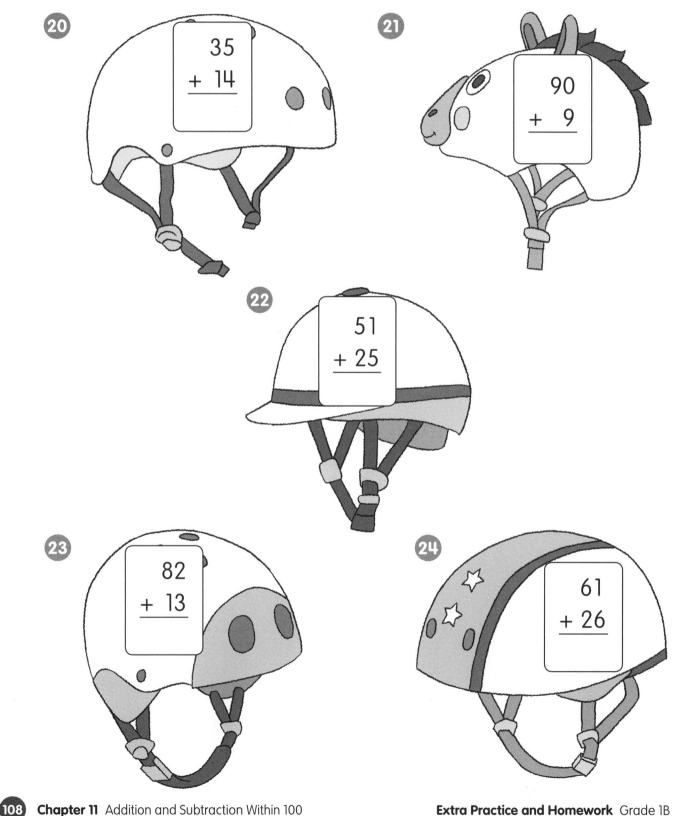

20

$$\begin{array}{r} 35 \\ + 14 \\ \hline \end{array}$$

21

$$\begin{array}{r} 90 \\ + 9 \\ \hline \end{array}$$

22

$$\begin{array}{r} 51 \\ + 25 \\ \hline \end{array}$$

23

$$\begin{array}{r} 82 \\ + 13 \\ \hline \end{array}$$

24

$$\begin{array}{r} 61 \\ + 26 \\ \hline \end{array}$$

© 2020 Marshall Cavendish Education Pte Ltd

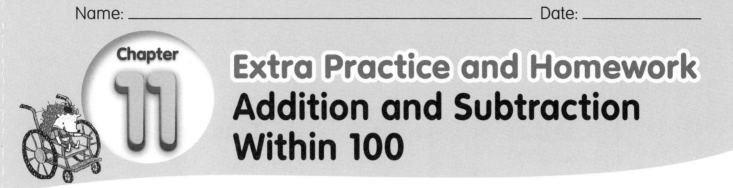

Chapter 11

Extra Practice and Homework
Addition and Subtraction Within 100

Activity 2   Addition With Regrouping

Add and regroup.

Example

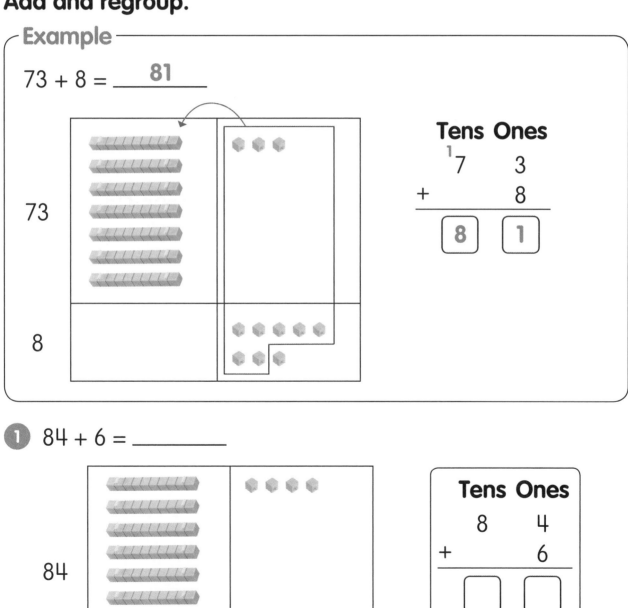

$73 + 8 = \underline{\quad 81 \quad}$

Tens	Ones
^{1}7	3
+	8
8	**1**

1   $84 + 6 = \underline{\qquad}$

Tens	Ones
8	4
+	6

© 2020 Marshall Cavendish Education Pte Ltd

2 67 + 9 = _____

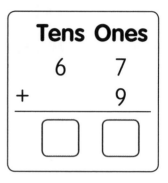

3 55 + 7 = _____

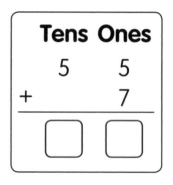

© 2020 Marshall Cavendish Education Pte Ltd

Add and regroup.
Match.

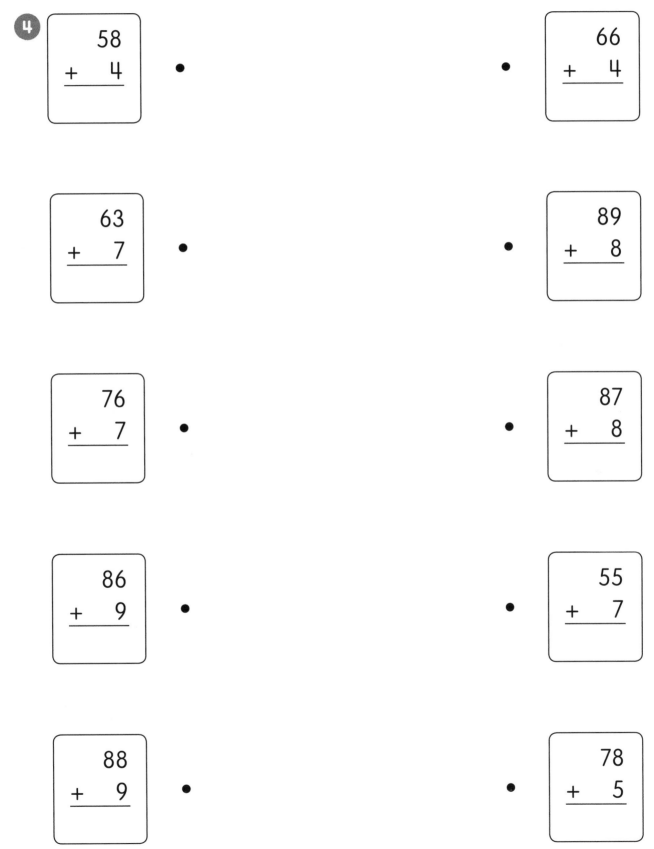

4

$$\begin{array}{r} 58 \\ + 4 \\ \hline \end{array}$$ •

$$\begin{array}{r} 63 \\ + 7 \\ \hline \end{array}$$ •

$$\begin{array}{r} 76 \\ + 7 \\ \hline \end{array}$$ •

$$\begin{array}{r} 86 \\ + 9 \\ \hline \end{array}$$ •

$$\begin{array}{r} 88 \\ + 9 \\ \hline \end{array}$$ •

• $$\begin{array}{r} 66 \\ + 4 \\ \hline \end{array}$$

• $$\begin{array}{r} 89 \\ + 8 \\ \hline \end{array}$$

• $$\begin{array}{r} 87 \\ + 8 \\ \hline \end{array}$$

• $$\begin{array}{r} 55 \\ + 7 \\ \hline \end{array}$$

• $$\begin{array}{r} 78 \\ + 5 \\ \hline \end{array}$$

© 2020 Marshall Cavendish Education Pte Ltd

Add and regroup.

Example

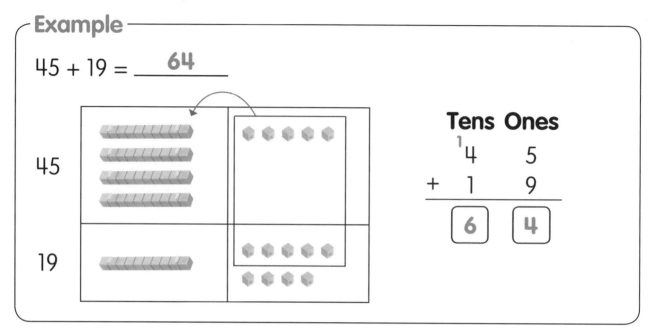

45 + 19 = _____64_____

Tens	Ones
¹4	5
+ 1	9
6	**4**

45

19

---

5 64 + 28 = _____

64

28

Tens	Ones
6	4
+ 2	8
☐	☐

© 2020 Marshall Cavendish Education Pte Ltd

6 46 + 35 = _____

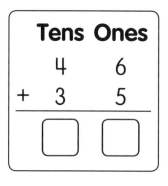

Tens	Ones
4	6
+ 3	5
☐	☐

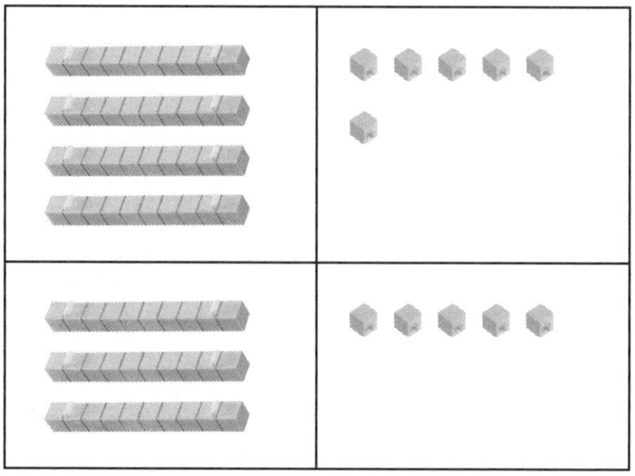

7 59 + 29 = _____

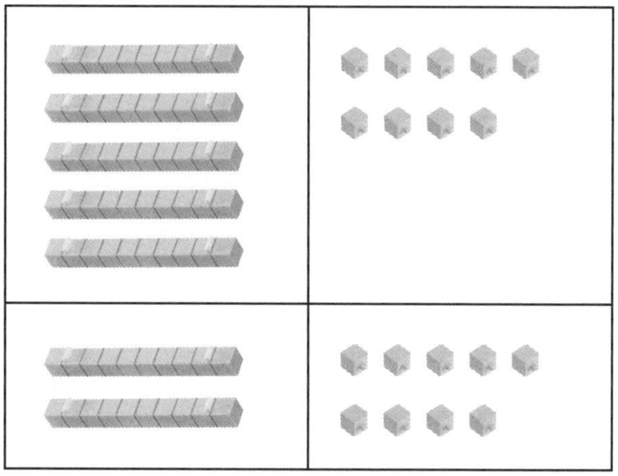

Tens	Ones
5	9
+ 2	9
☐	☐

© 2020 Marshall Cavendish Education Pte Ltd

The pairs of shoes are mixed up.
Add to find shoes with numbers that match.
Join them.

8

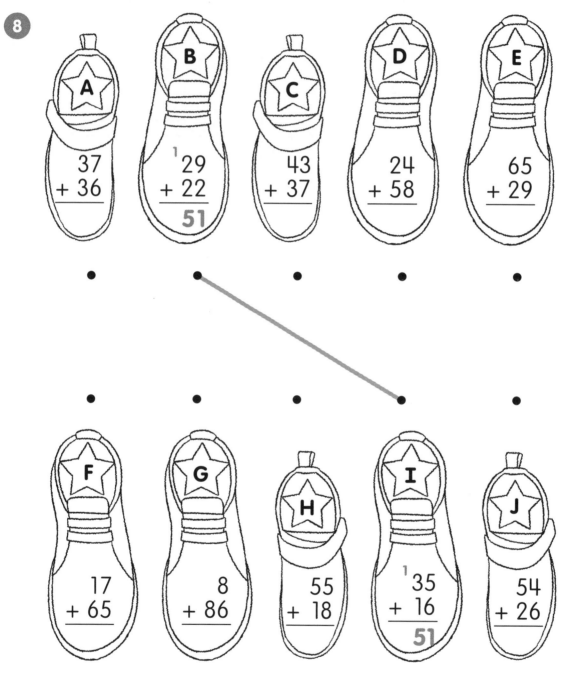

A
37
+ 36
___

B
¹29
+ 22
___
51

C
43
+ 37
___

D
24
+ 58
___

E
65
+ 29
___

F
17
+ 65
___

G
8
+ 86
___

H
55
+ 18
___

I
¹35
+ 16
___
51

J
54
+ 26
___

© 2020 Marshall Cavendish Education Pte Ltd

Add.

9 27 + 13 = _____

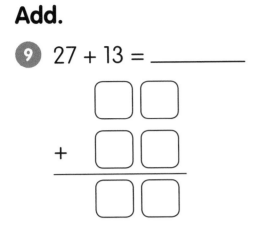

10 29 + 41 = _____

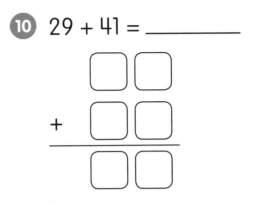

11 38 + 42 = _____

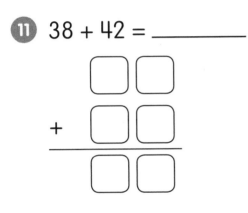

12 26 + 24 = _____

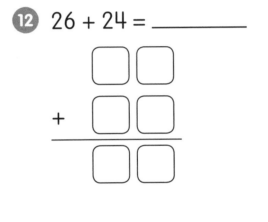

13 54 + 6 = _____

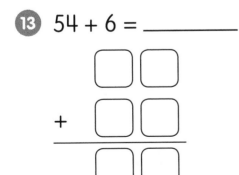

14 44 + 46 = _____

© 2020 Marshall Cavendish Education Pte Ltd

Add.

15 52 + 19 = _____ $\quad$ Y

16 58 + 6 = _____ $\quad$ B

17 67 + 18 = _____ $\quad$ A

18 48 + 38 = _____ $\quad$ E

19 43 + 57 = _____ $\quad$ R

20 39 + 49 = _____ $\quad$ T

21 27 + 49 = _____ $\quad$ D

Now, match each letter to the numbers below.
What toy is named after President Theodore Roosevelt?

| 88 | 86 | 76 | 76 | 71 | | 64 | 86 | 85 | 100 |

© 2020 Marshall Cavendish Education Pte Ltd

22 Ron drops a ball into a number machine.
Which ball is it?

Write the number in the ⬭.

© 2020 Marshall Cavendish Education Pte Ltd

Add.
Then, draw lines to match the same numbers.

23

98

52

80

56

60

73

29 + 44

28 + 28

64 + 16

35 + 17

26 + 34

39 + 59

© 2020 Marshall Cavendish Education Pte Ltd

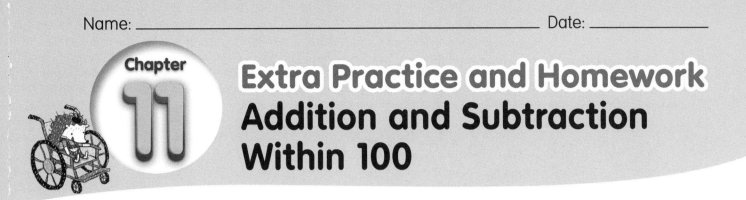

Activity 3   Subtraction Without Regrouping

Count back to subtract.
Count back from the greater number.
Then, fill in each blank.

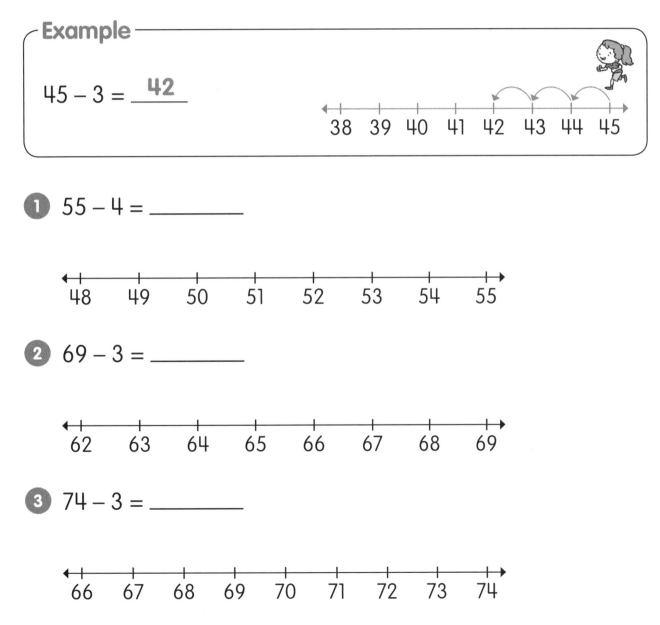

Example

$45 - 3 = \underline{\ 42\ }$

```
←+————+————+————+————+————+————+————+→
  38   39   40   41   42   43   44   45
```

1 $55 - 4 = \underline{\hspace{2cm}}$

```
←+————+————+————+————+————+————+————+→
  48    49    50    51    52    53    54    55
```

2 $69 - 3 = \underline{\hspace{2cm}}$

```
←+————+————+————+————+————+————+————+→
  62    63    64    65    66    67    68    69
```

3 $74 - 3 = \underline{\hspace{2cm}}$

```
←+————+————+————+————+————+————+————+→
  66   67   68   69   70   71   72   73   74
```

© 2020 Marshall Cavendish Education Pte Ltd

4 99 − 4 = _____

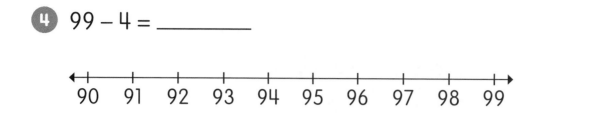

Subtract.

Example

	Tens	Ones
	4	5
−		3
	4	2

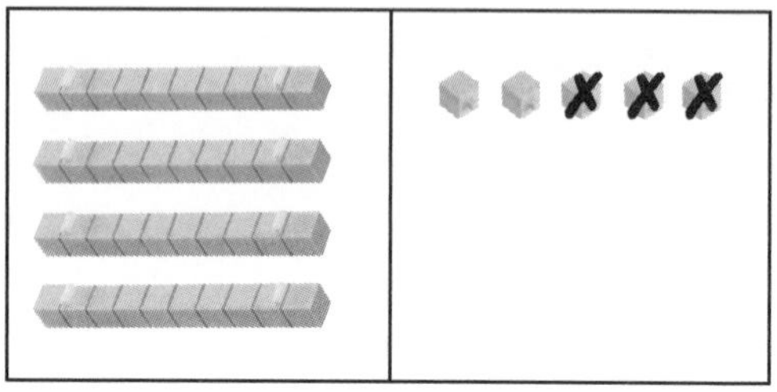

45 − 3 = __42__

5

	Tens	Ones
	6	9
−		6

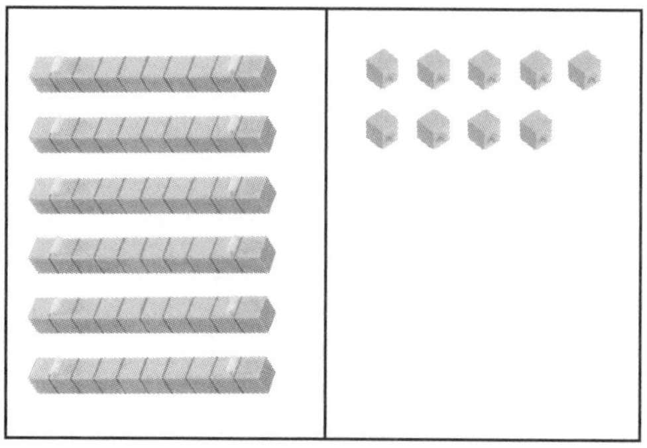

69 − 6 = _____

6

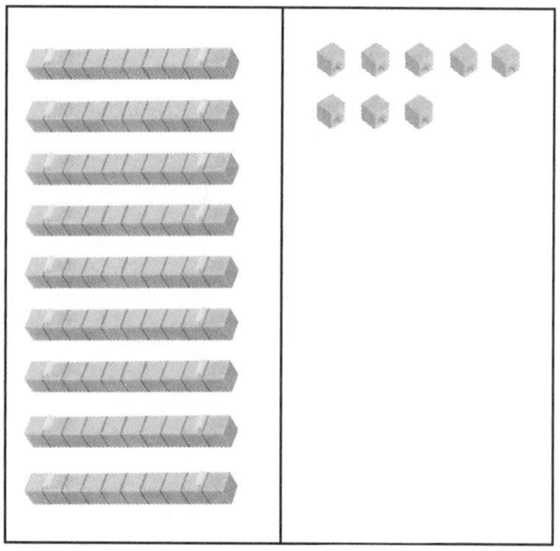

	Tens	Ones
	9	8
−		2

98 − 2 = _____

© 2020 Marshall Cavendish Education Pte Ltd

Count back by tens to subtract.
Count back from the greater number.
Then, fill in each blank.

© 2020 Marshall Cavendish Education Pte Ltd

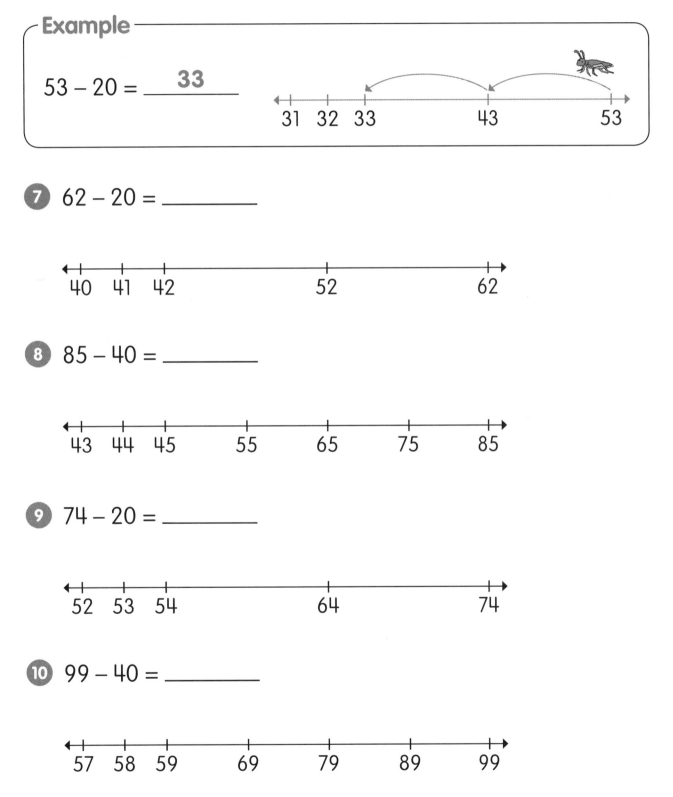

Example

$53 - 20 =$ _____ **33**

31 32 33   43   53

---

7 $62 - 20 =$ _____

40 41 42   52   62

---

8 $85 - 40 =$ _____

43 44 45 55 65 75 85

---

9 $74 - 20 =$ _____

52 53 54   64   74

---

10 $99 - 40 =$ _____

57 58 59 69 79 89 99

Subtract.

Example

83 − 50 = ____33____

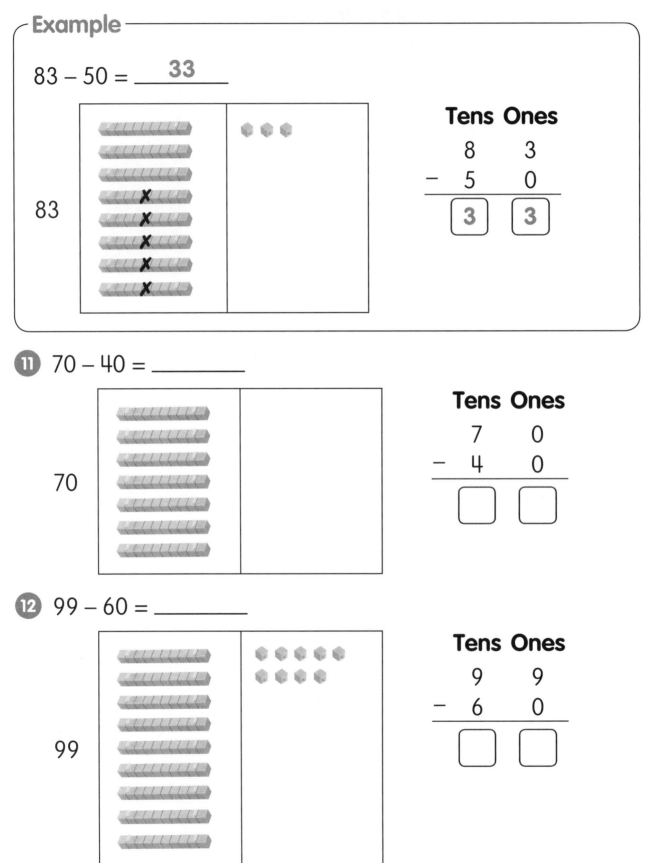

	Tens	Ones
	8	3
−	5	0
	3	3

11 70 − 40 = _____

	Tens	Ones
	7	0
−	4	0

12 99 − 60 = _____

	Tens	Ones
	9	9
−	6	0

© 2020 Marshall Cavendish Education Pte Ltd

$66 - 25 =$ _____41_____

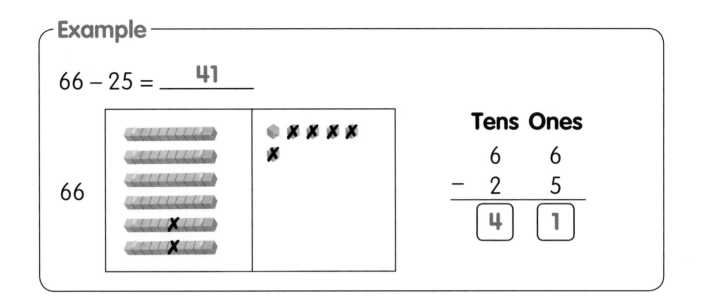

	Tens	Ones
	6	6
−	2	5
	4	**1**

---

13 $89 - 73 =$ _____

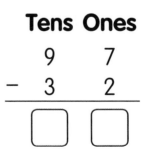

89

	Tens	Ones
	8	9
−	7	3
	☐	☐

---

14 $97 - 32 =$ _____

97

	Tens	Ones
	9	7
−	3	2
	☐	☐

© 2020 Marshall Cavendish Education Pte Ltd

Subtract.
Then, fill in each box.

15
$37 - 3$

16
$48 - 5$

17
$59 - 12$

18
$75 - 25$

19
$87 - 33$

20
$89 - 47$

© 2020 Marshall Cavendish Education Pte Ltd

21) 66 – 24

22) 99 – 68

23) 50 – 20

24) 90 – 60

25) 80 – 50

26) 90 – 90

© 2020 Marshall Cavendish Education Pte Ltd

Add.
Then, subtract.
Fill in each blank.

27

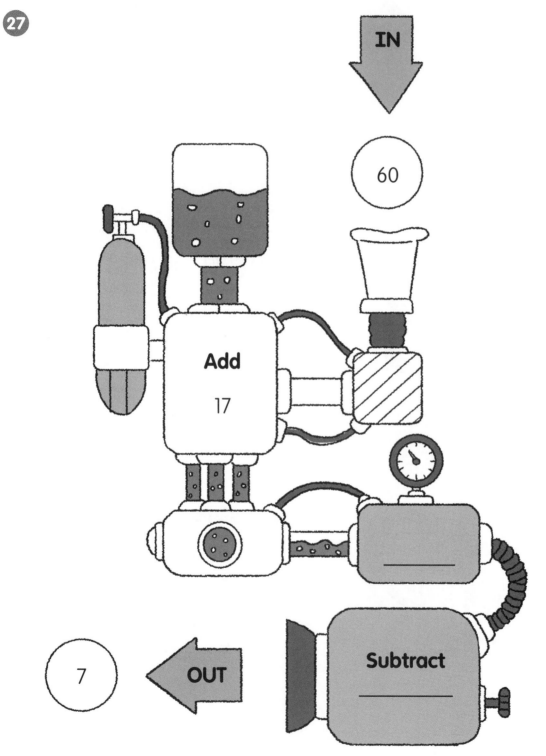

IN

60

Add

17

Subtract

_____

OUT

7

© 2020 Marshall Cavendish Education Pte Ltd

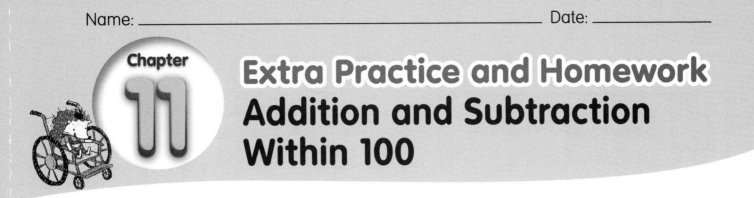

Activity 4   Subtraction With Regrouping

Regroup and subtract.

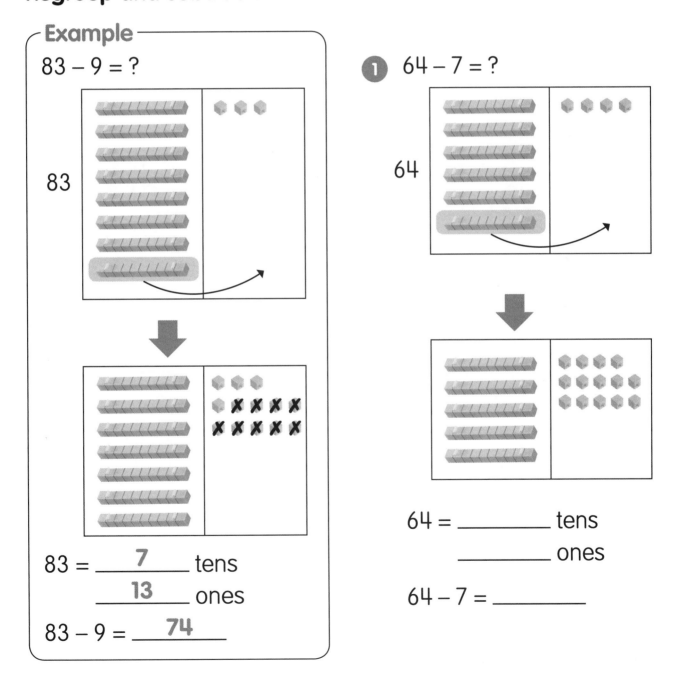

Example

83 – 9 = ?

83

83 = ___7___ tens
___13___ ones

83 – 9 = ___74___

1   64 – 7 = ?

64

64 = _____ tens
_____ ones

64 – 7 = _____

© 2020 Marshall Cavendish Education Pte Ltd

2 90 − 6 = ?

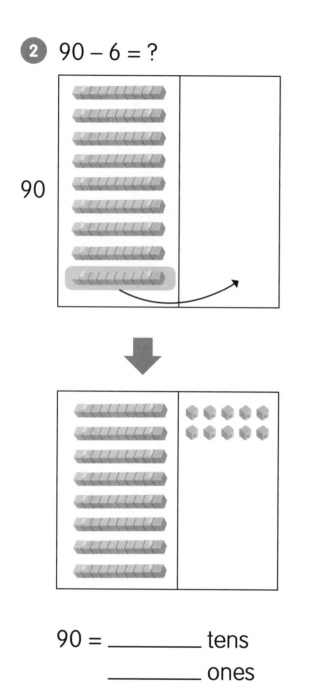

90

↓

90 = _____ tens
_____ ones

90 − 6 = _____

3 52 − 8 = ?

52

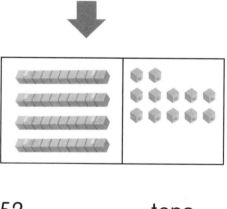

↓

52 = _____ tens
_____ ones

52 − 8 = _____

© 2020 Marshall Cavendish Education Pte Ltd

Subtract.
Then, draw lines to match the same numbers.

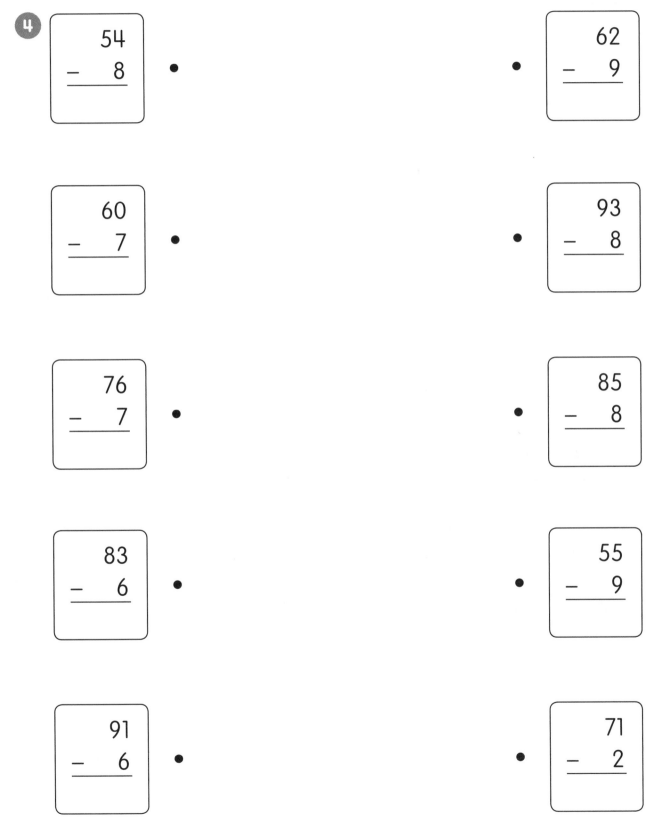

4

$$\begin{array}{r} 54 \\ -8 \\ \hline \end{array}$$

$$\begin{array}{r} 62 \\ -9 \\ \hline \end{array}$$

$$\begin{array}{r} 60 \\ -7 \\ \hline \end{array}$$

$$\begin{array}{r} 93 \\ -8 \\ \hline \end{array}$$

$$\begin{array}{r} 76 \\ -7 \\ \hline \end{array}$$

$$\begin{array}{r} 85 \\ -8 \\ \hline \end{array}$$

$$\begin{array}{r} 83 \\ -6 \\ \hline \end{array}$$

$$\begin{array}{r} 55 \\ -9 \\ \hline \end{array}$$

$$\begin{array}{r} 91 \\ -6 \\ \hline \end{array}$$

$$\begin{array}{r} 71 \\ -2 \\ \hline \end{array}$$

© 2020 Marshall Cavendish Education Pte Ltd

Regroup and subtract.

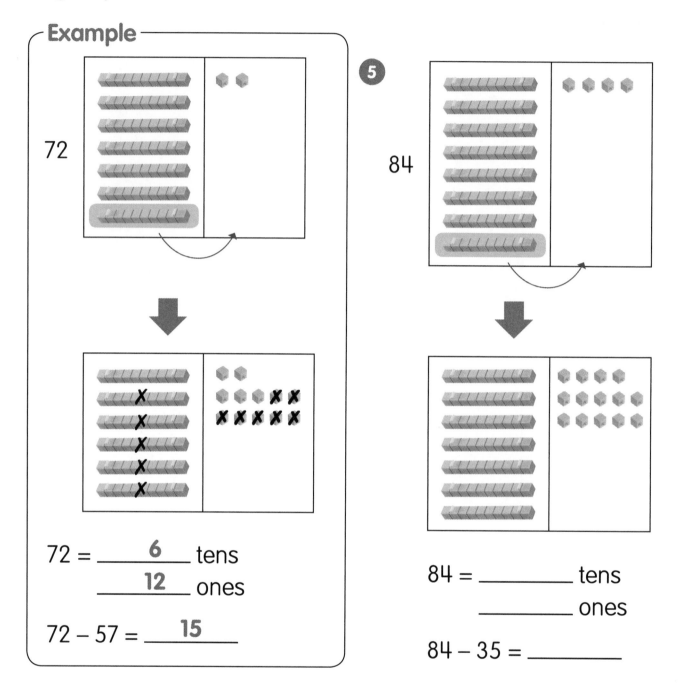

Example

72

$72 = \underline{\quad 6 \quad}$ tens
$\underline{\quad 12 \quad}$ ones

$72 - 57 = \underline{\quad 15 \quad}$

5

84

$84 = \underline{\qquad}$ tens
$\underline{\qquad}$ ones

$84 - 35 = \underline{\qquad}$

© 2020 Marshall Cavendish Education Pte Ltd

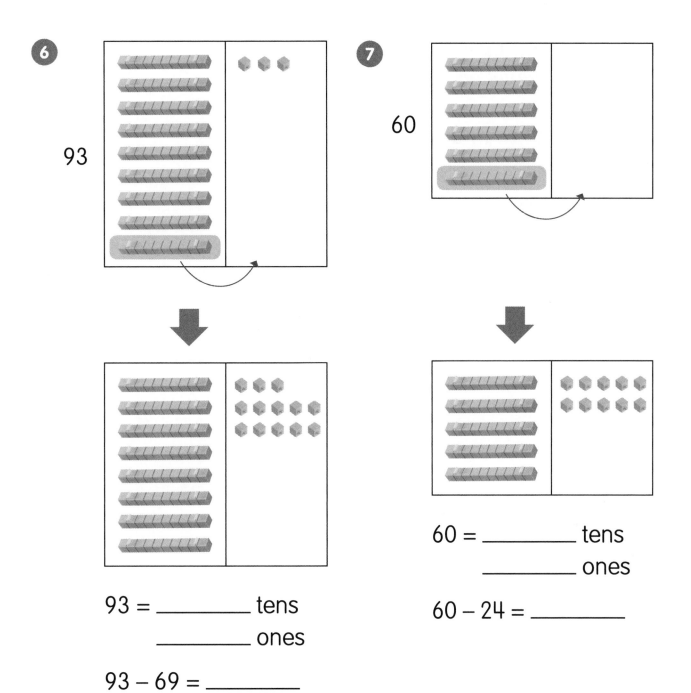

6

93

93 = _____ tens

_____ ones

93 − 69 = _____

7

60

60 = _____ tens

_____ ones

60 − 24 = _____

© 2020 Marshall Cavendish Education Pte Ltd

Five girls are going to a party.
Which dress will each girl wear?
Subtract.
Then, match to find out.

8 Emma   Ally   Tara   Carla   Bella

$$40 - 12$$ $$51 - 28$$ $$63 - 37$$ $$74 - 47$$ $$85 - 69$$

16   27   28   23   26

© 2020 Marshall Cavendish Education Pte Ltd

Subtract.
Then, draw lines to match the same numbers.

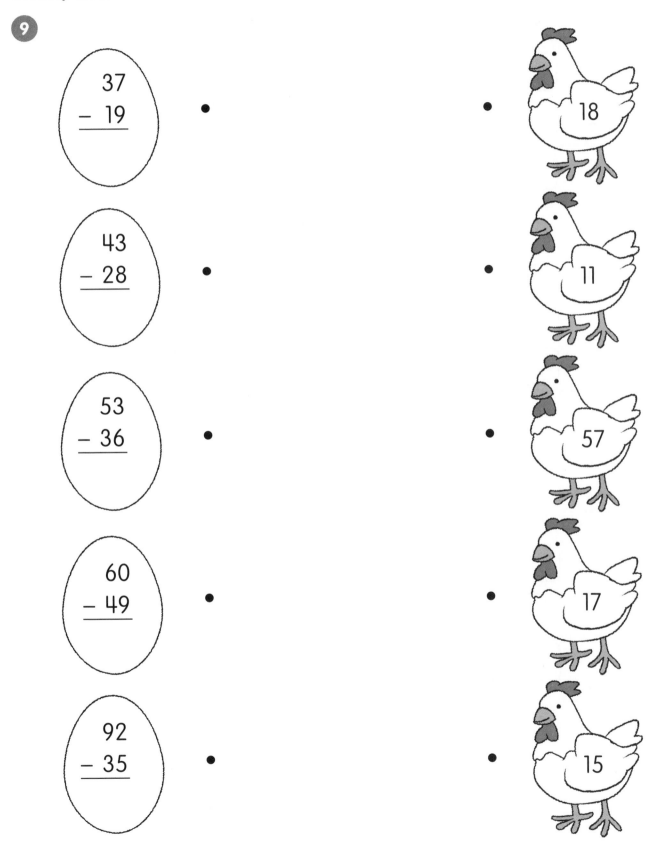

9

$$\begin{array}{r} 37 \\ -\ 19 \\ \hline \end{array}$$

$$\begin{array}{r} 43 \\ -\ 28 \\ \hline \end{array}$$

$$\begin{array}{r} 53 \\ -\ 36 \\ \hline \end{array}$$

$$\begin{array}{r} 60 \\ -\ 49 \\ \hline \end{array}$$

$$\begin{array}{r} 92 \\ -\ 35 \\ \hline \end{array}$$

18

11

57

17

15

© 2020 Marshall Cavendish Education Pte Ltd

Regroup and subtract.
Fill in each blank.

10 61 − 35 = _____

11 76 − 27 = _____

12 55 − 28 = _____

13 91 − 58 = _____

14 82 − 54 = _____

15 70 − 47 = _____

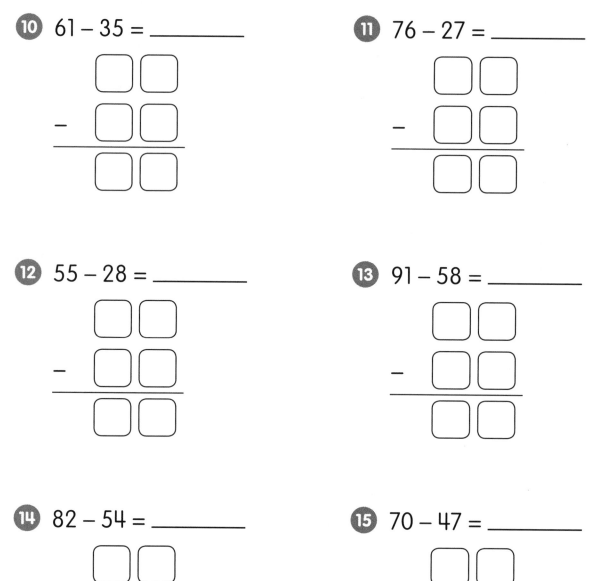

Extra Practice and Homework Grade 1B

© 2020 Marshall Cavendish Education Pte Ltd

Subtract.
Fill in each blank.

16 58 − 29 = _____ **W**

90 − 78 = _____ **E**

82 − 55 = _____ **S**

66 − 38 = _____ **S**

67 − 47 = _____ **E**

74 − 59 = _____ **A**

Now, match each letter to the numbers below.
Then, solve the riddle.

What goes up and comes down at the same time?

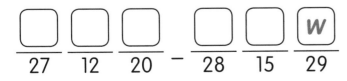

					W
27	12	20	− 28	15	29

© 2020 Marshall Cavendish Education Pte Ltd

Subtract.
Then, write the missing number in each blank.

17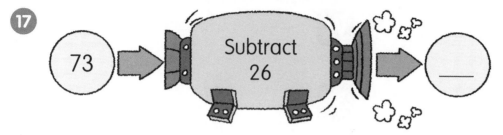

18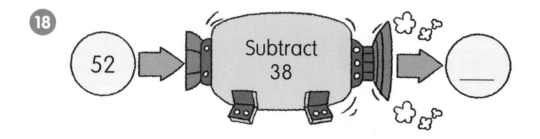

19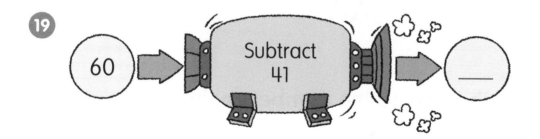

20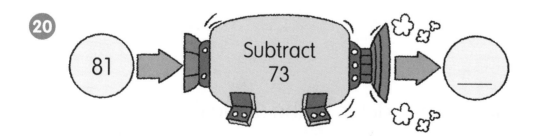

© 2020 Marshall Cavendish Education Pte Ltd

1 Mathematical Habit **2** Use mathematical reasoning

Look at the addition sentence and the table.
The steps to work out the addition sentence are
mixed up.
Number the steps in the correct order.

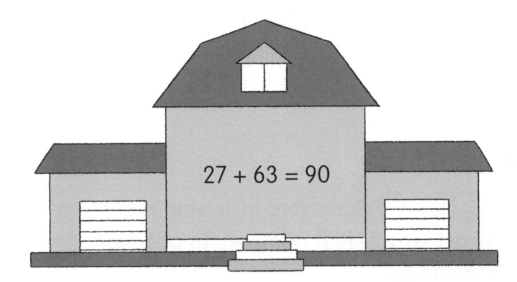

27 + 63 = 90

Number	Step
	7 ones + 3 ones = 10 ones
	Regroup the ones. 10 ones = 1 ten
	Add the tens.
1	Add the ones.
	1 ten + 2 tens + 6 tens = 9 tens

© 2020 Marshall Cavendish Education Pte Ltd

Mathematical Habit 1 Persevere in solving problems

1 **I add two 2-digit numbers to get 49.**
Fill in each box.

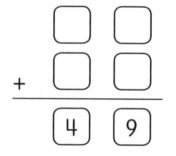

Mathematical Habit 1 Persevere in solving problems

2 **I subtract two 2-digit numbers to get 49.**
Fill in each box.

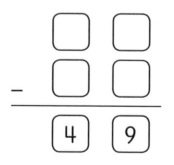

Check your answers to make sure they are 49.

© 2020 Marshall Cavendish Education Pte Ltd

SCHOOL-to-HOME CONNECTIONS

Chapter 12 — Graphs

Dear Family,

In this chapter, your child will learn to gather and show information in picture graphs.
Skills your child will practice include:
- interpreting picture graphs
- making tally charts
- representing information in tally charts as picture graphs

Math Practice

At the end of this chapter, you may want to carry out this activity with your child. This activity will help to strengthen your child's understanding of how to collect and represent information in a picture graph.

Activity

- Have your child conduct a survey of family members and friends to identify their favorite colors. Put the survey results in a **tally chart**, like the example below.

Favorite Color	Tally	Number
Blue	|||	3
Red	||	2
Green	|||||	5
Yellow			1

- Have your child make a picture graph to represent the data in his or her tally chart.

Math Talk

Discuss the following picture graph with your child. Talk about what the picture graph shows, and which pets received the **fewest** and the **most** votes. Also compare pairs of pets to determine which received **fewer** and **more** votes.

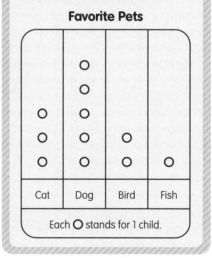

Favorite Pets

Cat · Dog · Bird · Fish

Each ◯ stands for 1 child.

© 2020 Marshall Cavendish Education Pte Ltd

BLANK

Extra Practice and Homework
Graphs

Activity 1   Simple Picture Graphs

Look at the picture graph.
Then, fill in each blank.

The picture graph shows the birth months of Aarón's friends.

Birth Months of Aarón's Friends

January	February	March

1 How many of Aarón's friends have their birthdays in January?

_____

2 In which month do most of Aarón's friends have their birthdays?

_____

© 2020 Marshall Cavendish Education Pte Ltd

Look at the picture graph.
Then, fill in each blank.

This picture graph shows all the toys in Taylor's toy box.

Toys in Taylor's Toy Box

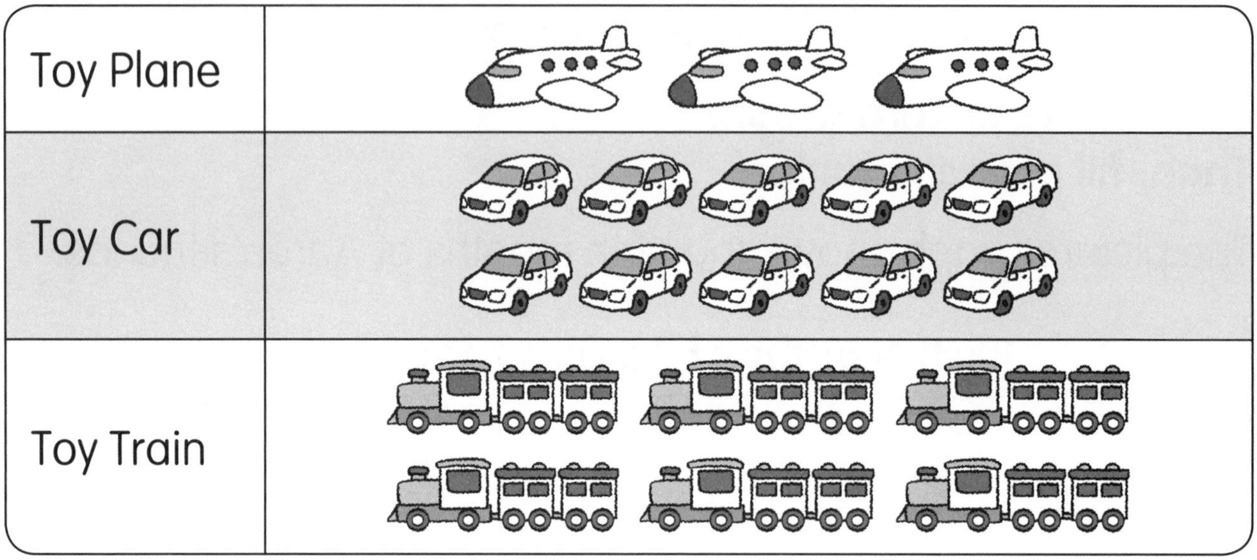

3 There are _____ toy planes in Taylor's toy box.

4 There are _____ toy cars.

5 There are _____ toy trains.

6 The number of _____ is the greatest.

7 The number of _____ is the least.

8 There are _____ more toy cars than toy trains.

9 There are 7 fewer _____ than toy cars.

© 2020 Marshall Cavendish Education Pte Ltd

Zane has a coin.
Every time he tosses the coin, he gets heads  or tails .
Zane tosses the coin many times.
This is what he gets:

Count the tosses for heads.
Color a ☐ for each toss.
Repeat the above for tails.

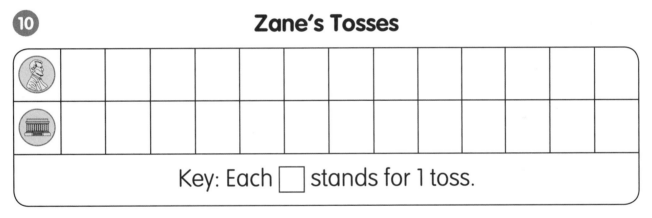

10   **Zane's Tosses**

Key: Each ☐ stands for 1 toss.

Use your graph to fill in each blank.

11 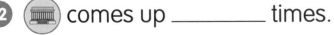 comes up _____ times.

12 comes up _____ times.

13 comes up _____ more times than .

© 2020 Marshall Cavendish Education Pte Ltd

This picture graph shows how a group of children goes to school.

Ways of Going to School

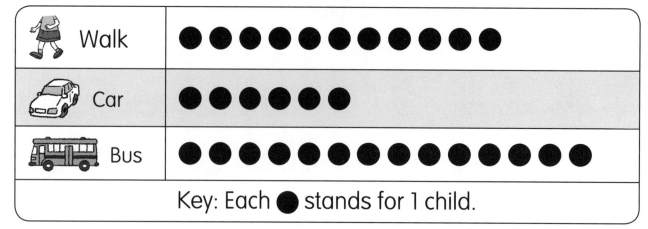

Key: Each ● stands for 1 child.

Look at the picture graph.
Then, fill in each blank.

⑭ How many children walk to school? _____

⑮ How many children go to school by bus? _____

⑯ Most of the children go to school by _____.

⑰ The least number of children go to school by

_____.

⑱ There are _____ more children who take the bus
than walk to school.

⑲ More children walk to school than go to school by car.

How many more? _____

⑳ Fewer children go to school by car than by bus.

How many fewer? _____

© 2020 Marshall Cavendish Education Pte Ltd

Name: ______________________ Date: ____________

Chapter 12 Extra Practice and Homework
Graphs

Activity 2 Tally Charts and Picture Graphs

There are some spoons, tea cups, and plates on the table.

1 Complete the tally chart.

Type of Tableware	Tally	Number
Spoon	𝍸	5
Tea Cup		
Plate		

© 2020 Marshall Cavendish Education Pte Ltd

Make a picture graph.
Use ☺ to stand for 1 item.

2   **Tableware on a Table**

🥄	Spoon	
☕	Tea Cup	
🍽	Plate	
Key: Each ☺ stands for 1 item.		

Fill in each blank.

3 How many spoons are there? _____

4 How many plates are there? _____

5 There are 2 more _____ than spoons.

6 There are _____ fewer plates than tea cups.

7 There are _____ items on the table in all.

© 2020 Marshall Cavendish Education Pte Ltd

Leah bought some balloons for her party.
The tally chart shows the different colors of balloons
she bought.

Complete the tally chart.

8

Color of Balloons	Tally	Number
Red	IIII I	
Blue	IIII IIII	
Yellow	IIII IIII IIII	

Make a picture graph.
Use △ to stand for 1 balloon.

9

Balloons for Leah's Party

Red	
Blue	
Yellow	

Key: Each △ stands for 1 balloon.

2 Tally Charts and Picture Graphs

© 2020 Marshall Cavendish Education Pte Ltd

Fill in each blank.

10 Leah bought _____ red balloons.

11 She bought _____ blue balloons.

12 She bought _____ yellow balloons.

13 She bought _____ more yellow balloons than

blue balloons.

14 She bought 9 fewer _____ balloons

than _____ balloons.

15 The number of _____ balloons is the most.

16 The number of _____ balloons is the least.

17 She bought _____ balloons in all.

© 2020 Marshall Cavendish Education Pte Ltd

Jess bought some seed packages.
The tally chart shows the different kinds of seeds she bought.

Complete the tally chart.

18

Kind of Seed Packages	Tally	Number
Cucumber	卌 ‖	
Pumpkin	‖‖	
Sunflower	卌	

Make a picture graph.
Draw ⬤ for each seed package.

19   **Seed Packages Jess Bought**

Cucumber	
Pumpkin	
Sunflower	

Key: Each ⬤ stands for 1 seed package.

© 2020 Marshall Cavendish Education Pte Ltd

Fill in each blank.

20 How many packages of sunflower seeds did Jess buy?

_____

21 How many packages of cucumber seeds did she buy?

_____

22 How many packages of pumpkin seeds did she buy?

_____

23 How many more packages of cucumber seeds than

pumpkin seeds did she buy? _____

24 How many packages of seeds did she buy in all?

_____

25 She bought 2 more packages of _____ seeds than
pumpkin seeds.

© 2020 Marshall Cavendish Education Pte Ltd

Ryan invites his friends to a party.
5 children drink orange juice.
1 more child drinks apple juice than orange juice.
2 fewer children drink grape juice than apple juice.

Make a tally chart.

Type of Fruit Juice	Tally	Number
Orange		
Grape		
Apple		

26 (row label)

Make a picture graph.
Use to stand for 1 child.

27   **Fruit Juices at the Party**

Orange	
Grape	
Apple	

Key: Each stands for 1 child.

2 Tally Charts and Picture Graphs

© 2020 Marshall Cavendish Education Pte Ltd

28 _____ children drink grape juice.

29 _____ children drink apple juice.

30 _____ children drink orange juice.

31 _____ juice is the most popular.

32 _____ juice is the least popular.

33 There are _____ fewer children who drink grape juice than apple juice.

34 _____ children drink the fruit juices at the party in all.

© 2020 Marshall Cavendish Education Pte Ltd

Mathematical Habit 6 Use precise mathematical language

Keep a record of how many books you read this week.
Include the books you read in class and those your teacher or your family reads to you.
Make a picture graph.
Use 📖 to stand for 1 book.

1 **Number of Books I Read This Week**

Sunday	Monday	Tuesday	Wednesday	Thursday	Friday	Saturday

Key: Each 📖 stands for 1 book.

Look at your graph.
Write sentences about the number of books you have read.
You may use the words below.

2 more than   less than   most   fewest

_____

_____

_____

© 2020 Marshall Cavendish Education Pte Ltd

Mathematical Habit 1 Persevere in solving problems

1 Bruno and his friends play a game.
Bruno draws a picture graph to show all the scores.
He spills some milk over the graph.

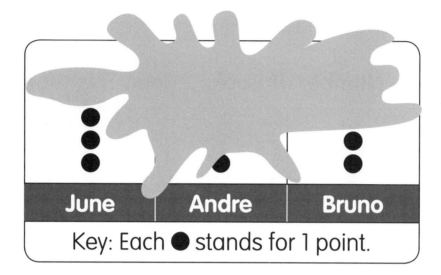

June Andre Bruno

Key: Each ● stands for 1 point.

Use the clues to find each child's score.

- The highest score is 6.
- Bruno does not have the highest score.
- The total score of all the children is 15 points.
- Bruno scores 1 more point than June.

Draw the correct number of ● above each name.

June	Andre	Bruno

Key: Each ● stands for 1 point.

© 2020 Marshall Cavendish Education Pte Ltd

Mathematical Habit **1** **Persevere in solving problems**

2 Tiana and her friends, Lola and Pedro, brought some bags of cookies to school.

Lola brought the least number of bags of cookies.

I brought 4 more bags of cookies than Lola.

Pedro brought 2 fewer bags of cookies than Tiana. He brought 5 bags of cookies.

Pedro   Tiana   Lola

Fill in the names and complete the tally chart.

a

Children	Tally	Number of Bags of Cookies

© 2020 Marshall Cavendish Education Pte Ltd

Make a picture graph.
Use ☐ to stand for 1 bag of cookies.

b   **Bags of Cookies the Children Brought to School**

Tiana	Lola	Pedro

Key: Each ☐ stands for 1 bag of cookies.

c   How many more bags of cookies did Pedro bring than

Lola? _____

d   How many bags of cookies did the children bring in all?

_____

© 2020 Marshall Cavendish Education Pte Ltd

SCHOOL-to-HOME
CONNECTIONS

Chapter 13

Money

Dear Family,

In this chapter, your child will learn about coins. Skills your child will practice include:
- identifying pennies, nickels, dimes, quarters
- finding the total value of a set of coins
- adding and subtracting money amounts

Math Practice

At the end of this chapter, you may want to carry out these activities with your child. These activities will help to strengthen your child's understanding of money.

Activity 1

- Gather play coins, and a paper bag.
- Put the coins in the bag, and take turns playing *How Much Am I?*.
- Withdraw some coins from the bag.
- Have your child count the total amount of money that is withdrawn from the bag.
- Return the coins to the bag before your child leads the next round.

Activity 2

- Visit a library and read books about time and money, such as *Follow the Money* by Loreen Leedy; *One Cent, Two Cents, Old Cent, New Cent: All About Money* by Bonnie Worth; and *Once Upon a Dime: A Math Adventure* by Nancy Kelly Allen.

Activity 3

- Go online to find videos available on the Internet that will help your child learn the values of coins.
- Ask your child to select his or her favorite coin song and sing together.

Math Talk

Use play or real money to discuss the value of a penny, nickel, dime, and quarter. Invite your child to choose coins or a combination of coins to make a set of money, count the set's total value, and write the value using symbols, such as 39¢.

© 2020 Marshall Cavendish Education Pte Ltd

BLANK

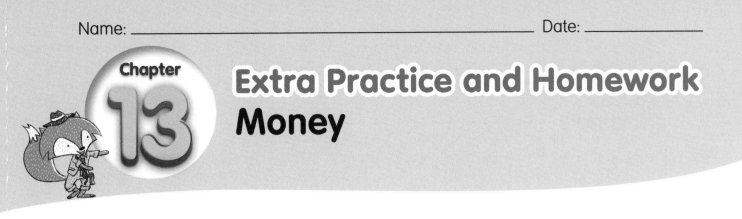

Chapter 13 Extra Practice and Homework
Money

Activity 1 Penny, Nickel, and Dime

Match.

1 •   • penny

       •   • nickel

       •   • dime

© 2020 Marshall Cavendish Education Pte Ltd

Write the value of each coin.

© 2020 Marshall Cavendish Education Pte Ltd

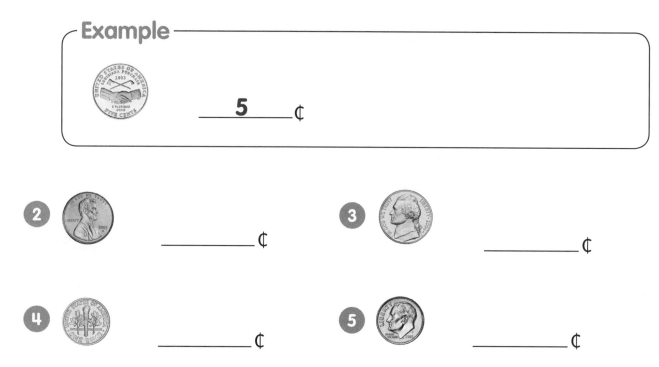

Example

_____**5**_____ ¢

2 _____ ¢

3 _____ ¢

4 _____ ¢

5 _____ ¢

Complete the table.

6

Type of Coins	Value	Name
Five cent	5¢	nickel
Ten cent		
One cent		

Extra Practice and Homework Grade 1B

Keisha has these coins.

Count the pennies, nickels, and dimes.
Then, fill in each blank.

7 There are _____ dimes.

8 There are _____ coins in all.

9 There are _____ fewer dimes than nickels.

10 There are _____ more pennies than dimes.

11 The value of the pennies is _____ ¢.

12 The value of the nickels is _____ ¢.

13 The value of the dimes is _____ ¢.

© 2020 Marshall Cavendish Education Pte Ltd

Write each missing number.

14

Count on by _____s.

_____, _____, _____, _____, _____,

_____, _____, _____ cents

There are _____ ¢.

15

Count on by _____s.

_____, _____, _____, _____, _____,

_____, _____ cents

There are _____ ¢.

16

Count on by _____s.

_____, _____, _____, _____, _____,

_____ cents

There are _____ ¢.

© 2020 Marshall Cavendish Education Pte Ltd

Find the value.

© 2020 Marshall Cavendish Education Pte Ltd

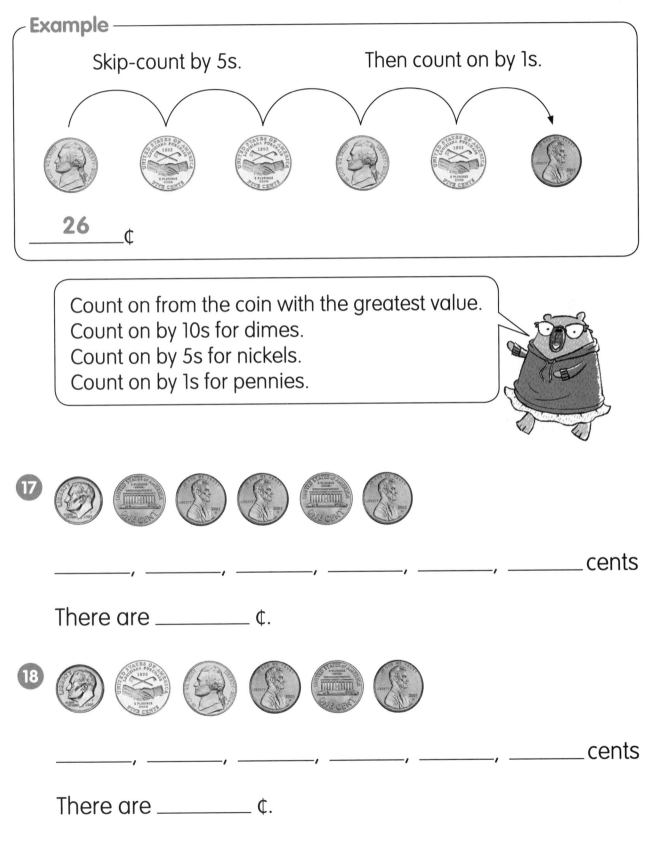

Example

Skip-count by 5s.   Then count on by 1s.

__26__ ¢

Count on from the coin with the greatest value.
Count on by 10s for dimes.
Count on by 5s for nickels.
Count on by 1s for pennies.

17

_____, _____, _____, _____, _____, _____ cents

There are _____ ¢.

18

_____, _____, _____, _____, _____, _____ cents

There are _____ ¢.

Write each missing number.

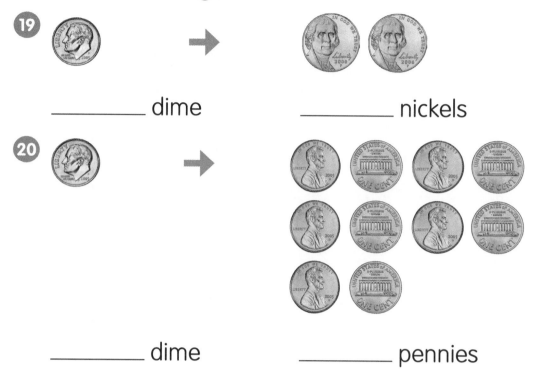

19

_____ dime

_____ nickels

20

_____ dime

_____ pennies

Solve the riddle.
Circle the correct coin.

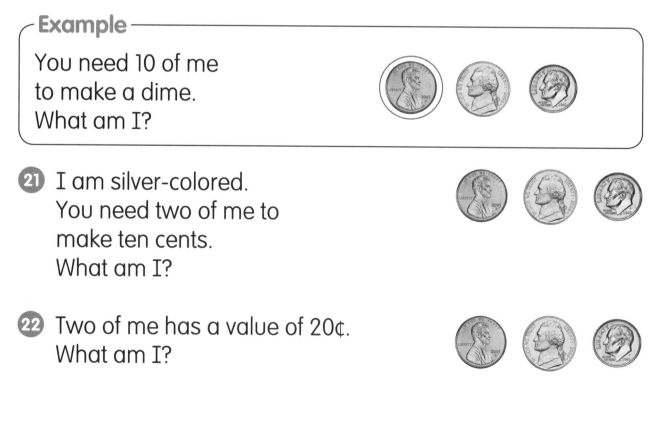

Example

You need 10 of me
to make a dime.
What am I?

21 I am silver-colored.
You need two of me to
make ten cents.
What am I?

22 Two of me has a value of 20¢.
What am I?

© 2020 Marshall Cavendish Education Pte Ltd

Find how many of each coin are needed.
Fill in each blank.

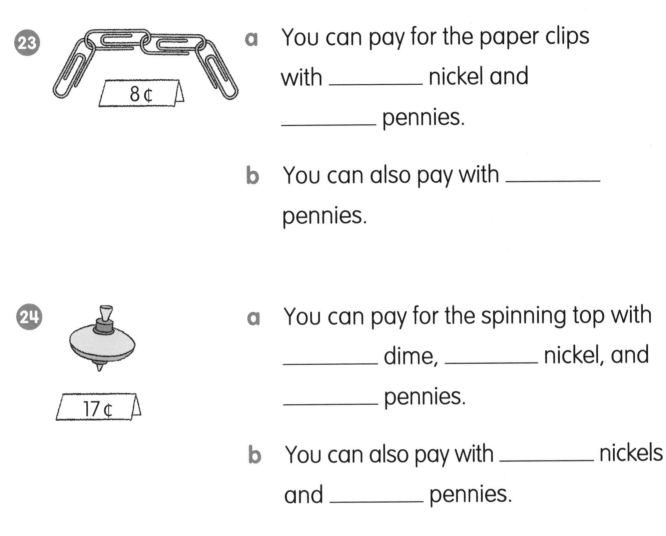

23

a You can pay for the paper clips with _____ nickel and _____ pennies.

b You can also pay with _____ pennies.

24

a You can pay for the spinning top with _____ dime, _____ nickel, and _____ pennies.

b You can also pay with _____ nickels and _____ pennies.

25

a You can pay for the paper mask with _____ dime, _____ nickels, and _____ pennies.

b You can also pay with _____ pennies.

© 2020 Marshall Cavendish Education Pte Ltd

Draw pennies (1¢)**, nickels** (5¢)**, and dimes** (10¢)**.**
Show each price in two different ways.

26	 9¢	**1st way** **2nd way**
27	 18¢	**1st way** **2nd way**
28	 23¢	**1st way** **2nd way**

© 2020 Marshall Cavendish Education Pte Ltd

Activity 2 Quarter

Fill in each blank.

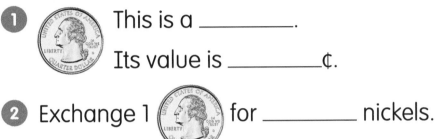

1 This is a _____.

   Its value is _____¢.

2 Exchange 1 [quarter] for _____ nickels.

Circle coins that can be exchanged for a quarter.

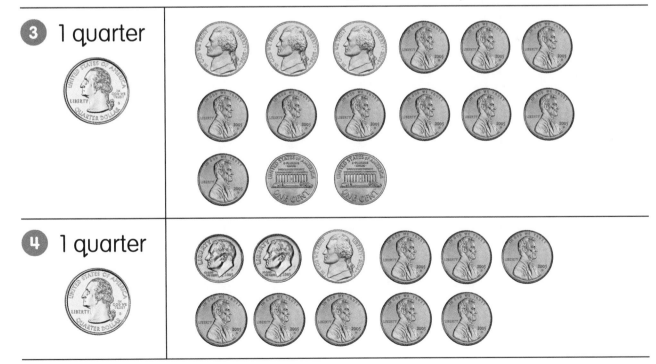

3 1 quarter

4 1 quarter

© 2020 Marshall Cavendish Education Pte Ltd

5 Draw pennies $\left(1¢\right)$, nickels $\left(5¢\right)$, dimes $\left(10¢\right)$, and quarters $\left(25¢\right)$.

Show five ways to pay for the keychain.

25 ¢

1st Way	
2nd Way	
3rd Way	
4th Way	
5th Way	

© 2020 Marshall Cavendish Education Pte Ltd

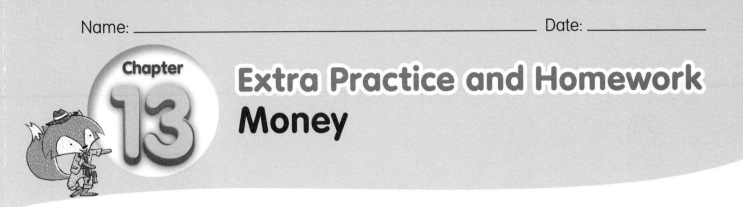

Chapter 13 Extra Practice and Homework
Money

Activity 3   Counting Money

Count on to find each amount of money.

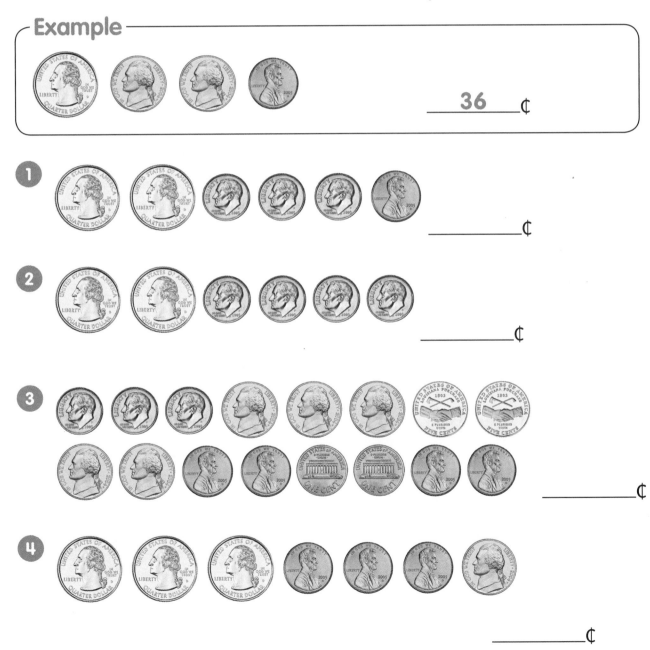

Example

36 ¢

1 _____ ¢

2 _____ ¢

3 _____ ¢

4 _____ ¢

5 **Match the correct amount to each item.**

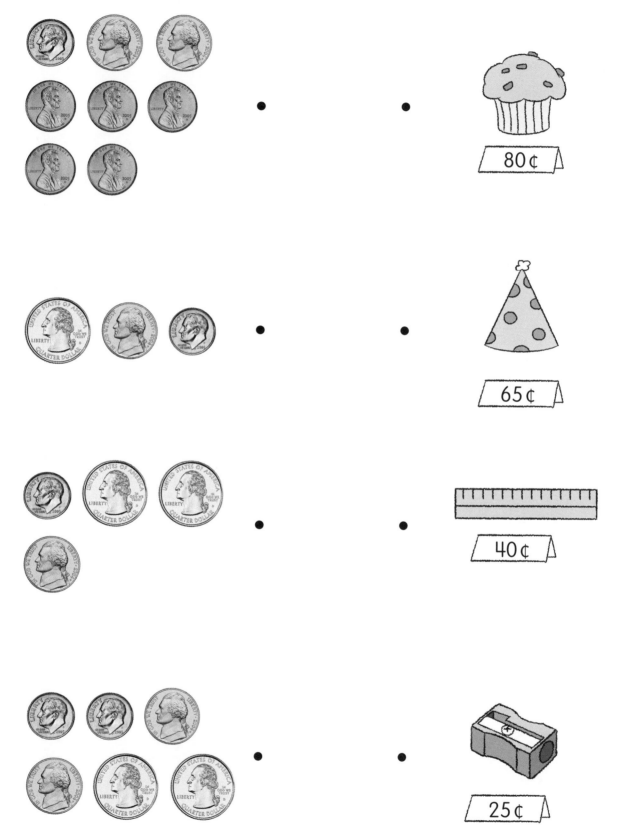

© 2020 Marshall Cavendish Education Pte Ltd

Circle the coins you need to pay for each item.

© 2020 Marshall Cavendish Education Pte Ltd

Example

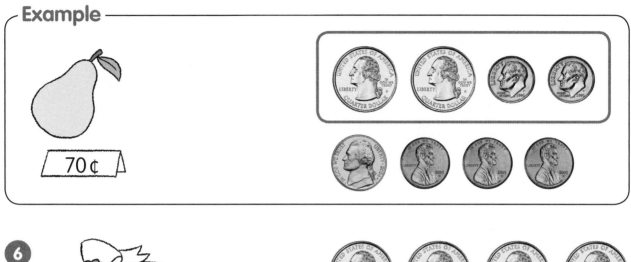

70¢

6

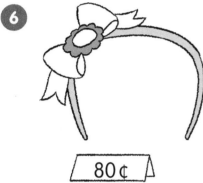

80¢

7

60¢

8

65¢

9

50¢

10

19¢

© 2020 Marshall Cavendish Education Pte Ltd

11

| 35 ¢ |

12

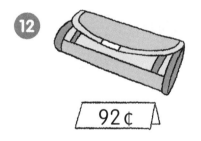

| 92 ¢ |

© 2020 Marshall Cavendish Education Pte Ltd

Draw pennies (1¢), nickels (5¢), dimes (10¢), and quarters (25¢) to show the given amount.

Start with the coin of the greatest value.

13 75¢

14 98¢

Draw pennies (1¢), nickels (5¢), dimes (10¢), and quarters (25¢).

Show two different ways to pay for the balloon.

15

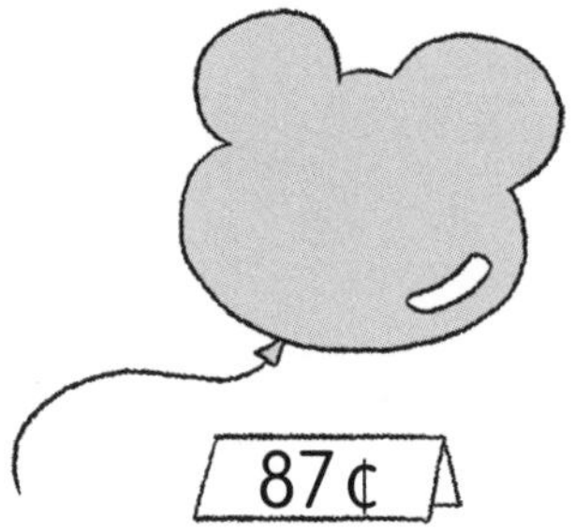

87¢

1st way
2nd way

© 2020 Marshall Cavendish Education Pte Ltd

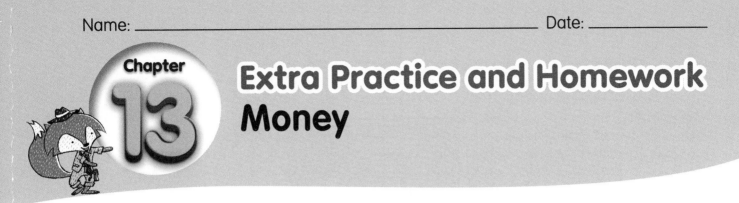

Chapter 13 **Extra Practice and Homework**
Money

Activity 4　Adding and Subtracting Money

Add.

Example

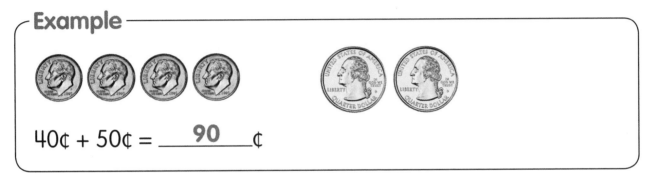

$40¢ + 50¢ = \underline{\quad 90 \quad}¢$

1

$25¢ + 19¢ = \underline{\qquad}¢$

2

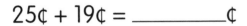

$45¢ + 15¢ = \underline{\qquad}¢$

© 2020 Marshall Cavendish Education Pte Ltd

The Art Club made cards to sell.

Fill in each blank.

Example

Tomas buys 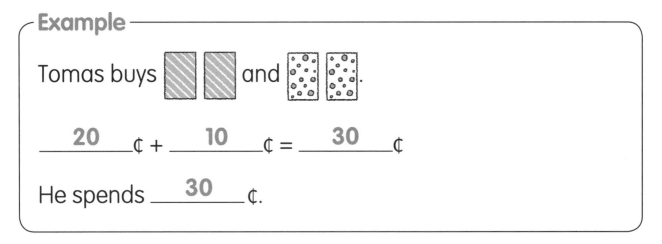 and .

_____20_____ ¢ + _____10_____ ¢ = _____30_____ ¢

He spends _____30_____ ¢.

© 2020 Marshall Cavendish Education Pte Ltd

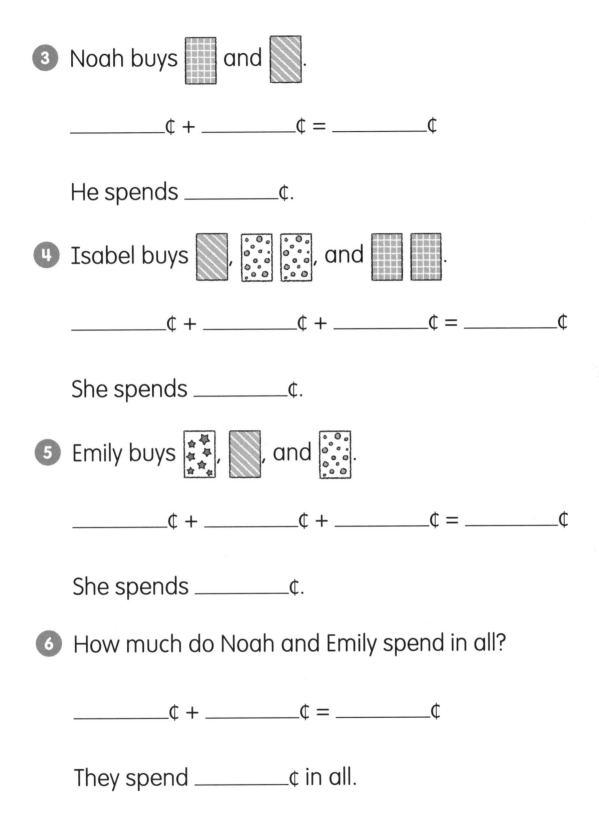

3 Noah buys ▦ and ▨.

_____¢ + _____¢ = _____¢

He spends _____¢.

4 Isabel buys ▨, ⬚ ⬚, and ▦ ▦.

_____¢ + _____¢ + _____¢ = _____¢

She spends _____¢.

5 Emily buys ✦, ▨, and ⬚.

_____¢ + _____¢ + _____¢ = _____¢

She spends _____¢.

6 How much do Noah and Emily spend in all?

_____¢ + _____¢ = _____¢

They spend _____¢ in all.

© 2020 Marshall Cavendish Education Pte Ltd

Add or subtract.

7 55¢ + 20¢ = _____¢

8 45¢ + 15¢ = _____¢

9 60¢ – 5¢ = _____¢

10 99¢ – 35¢ = _____¢

Answer each question.

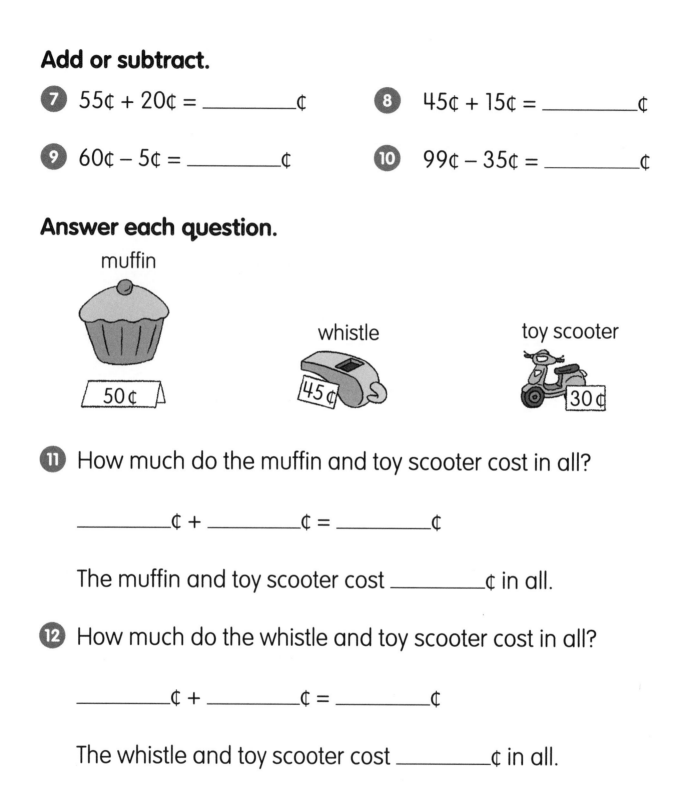

muffin

50 ¢

whistle

45 ¢

toy scooter

30 ¢

11 How much do the muffin and toy scooter cost in all?

_____¢ + _____¢ = _____¢

The muffin and toy scooter cost _____¢ in all.

12 How much do the whistle and toy scooter cost in all?

_____¢ + _____¢ = _____¢

The whistle and toy scooter cost _____¢ in all.

© 2020 Marshall Cavendish Education Pte Ltd

Solve.

You Have	You Buy	Your Change
Example quarter (25¢)	stamp 5¢	25¢ − 5¢ = 20¢
13 New York quarter, dime, dime, dime	muffin 50¢	
14 quarter, quarter	toy scooter 30¢	
15 quarter, quarter, quarter, dime	kite 80¢	
16 quarter, quarter	whistle 45¢	

© 2020 Marshall Cavendish Education Pte Ltd

Solve.

17 Adam buys a pen and a doll.
How much does he spend in all?

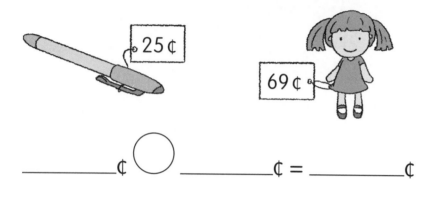

_____ ¢ ◯ _____ ¢ = _____ ¢

Adam spends _____ ¢ in all

18 Julia buys a ball.
She pays with three quarters.
How much change does she receive?

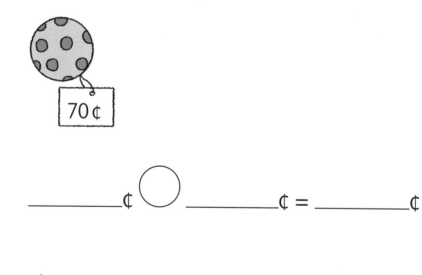

_____ ¢ ◯ _____ ¢ = _____ ¢

She receives _____ ¢ change.

© 2020 Marshall Cavendish Education Pte Ltd

Solve.

19 Alma has 90¢.
She buys a paper bag.
How much does she have left?

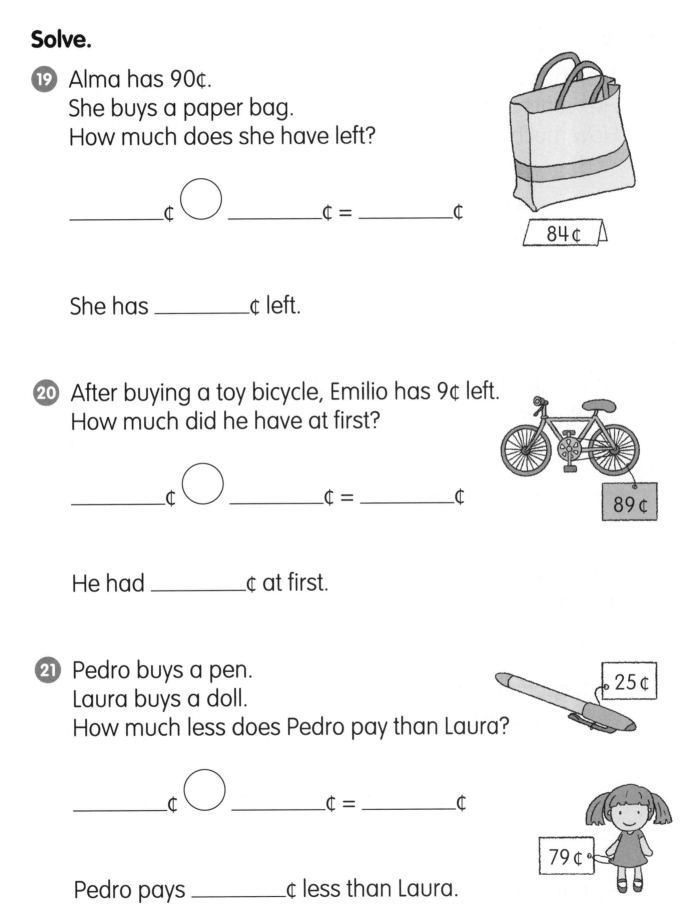

84¢

_____¢ ◯ _____¢ = _____¢

She has _____¢ left.

20 After buying a toy bicycle, Emilio has 9¢ left.
How much did he have at first?

89¢

_____¢ ◯ _____¢ = _____¢

He had _____¢ at first.

21 Pedro buys a pen.
Laura buys a doll.
How much less does Pedro pay than Laura?

25¢

_____¢ ◯ _____¢ = _____¢

79¢

Pedro pays _____¢ less than Laura.

© 2020 Marshall Cavendish Education Pte Ltd

Solve.

22 Ivan has 32¢.
He wants to buy a toy bicycle.
How much more does he need?

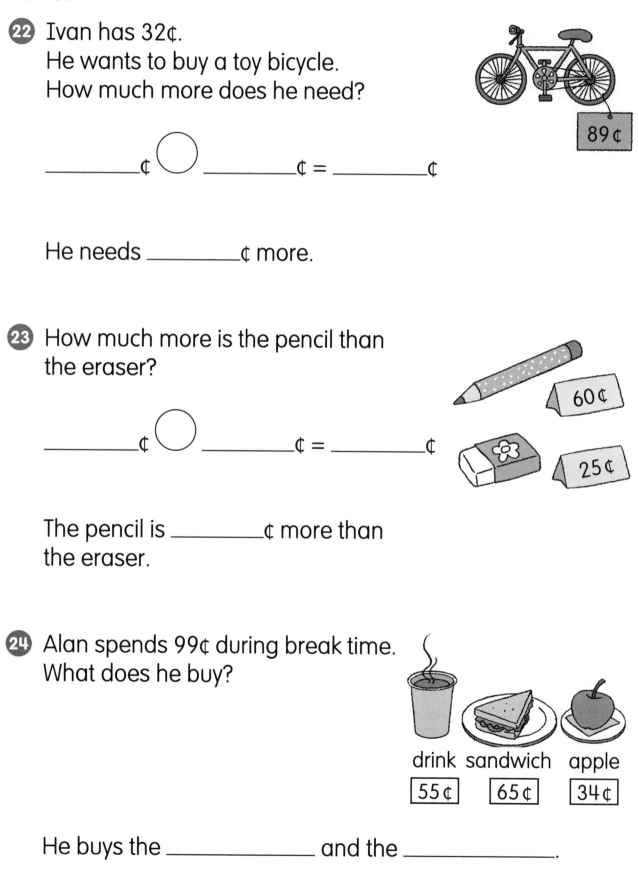

89 ¢

_____¢ ◯ _____¢ = _____¢

He needs _____¢ more.

23 How much more is the pencil than
the eraser?

60 ¢

25 ¢

_____¢ ◯ _____¢ = _____¢

The pencil is _____¢ more than
the eraser.

24 Alan spends 99¢ during break time.
What does he buy?

drink   sandwich   apple
55¢   65¢   34¢

He buys the _____ and the _____.

© 2020 Marshall Cavendish Education Pte Ltd

Jayden and Hana are at the cafeteria.

orange
30¢

crackers
20¢

cereal
50¢

muffin
65¢

25 Jayden uses two quarters to buy an orange.
How much change does he get?

_____¢ ◯ _____¢ = _____¢

He gets _____¢ change.

26 Hana has 3 dimes.
She buys her food and has 10¢ left.
What does she buy?

She buys _____.

© 2020 Marshall Cavendish Education Pte Ltd

Name: _____ Date: _____

Mathematical Habit 6 Use precise mathematical language

Elena and Hugo place all their money on a table.

**Write four sentences about the money.
An example has been done for you.**

1 There are eight dimes.

_____

_____

2 _____

_____

3 _____

_____

4 _____

_____

© 2020 Marshall Cavendish Education Pte Ltd

Mathematical Habit 1 Persevere in solving problems

1 Samuel wants to buy these drinks.

I am buying these drinks for Yong and Zara.

Orange juice 30¢   Apple juice 20¢

He uses four coins.
Draw the coins Samuel uses.

© 2020 Marshall Cavendish Education Pte Ltd

Mathematical Habit 1 Persevere in solving problems

2 Michael wants to buy a balloon for 45¢.
He has quarters, dimes, and nickels.
He can make 45¢ in 8 ways.

Write the correct number of coins.

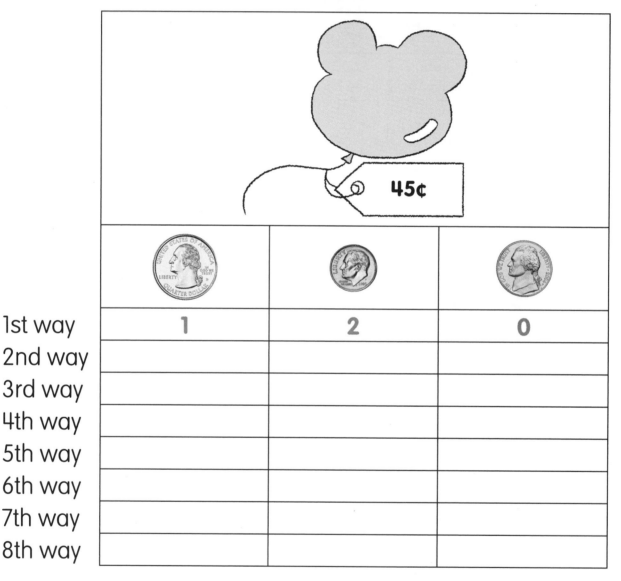

1st way	1	2	0
2nd way			
3rd way			
4th way			
5th way			
6th way			
7th way			
8th way			

The first way is 1 quarter and 2 dimes.

© 2020 Marshall Cavendish Education Pte Ltd